SUMMERS WITH
THE BEARS

SUMMERS WITH

THE BEARS

Six Seasons in the
North Woods

JACK BECKLUND
Photos by Patti and Jack Becklund

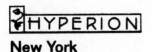
HYPERION
New York

Copyright © 1999, Jack Becklund.

Illustrations by Karralee Hammes

Photographs by Patti and Jack Becklund

Designed by Nancy Singer Olaguera

Library of Congress Cataloging-In-Publication Data

Becklund, Jack.
    Summers with the bears : six seasons in the north
  woods / Jack Becklund ; photos by Patti and Jack
  Becklund.
        p. cm.
   ISBN 0-7868-6393-5
   1. Black Bear—Minnesota—Anecdotes. 2. Becklund,
Jack. I. Title.
QL737.C27B4345 1998
599.78'5'09776—dc21
                                        98-10908
                                         CIP

Paperback ISBN 0-7868-8537-8

FIRST PAPERBACK EDITION

10 9 8 7 6 5 4 3 2 1

This book is dedicated to my wife, Patti, full partner and primary character in this enterprise. If not for her personal efforts, the amazing bears would have remained strangers, and the words to describe them unwritten.

CONTENTS

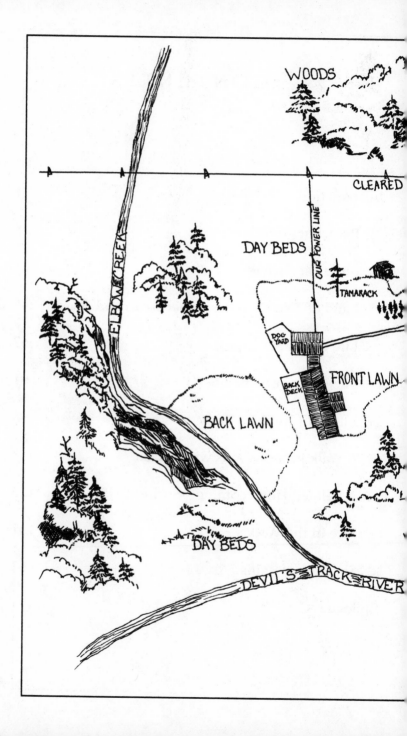

WOODS

CLEARED

DAY BEDS

ELBOW CREEK

OUR POWER LINE

TAMARACK

DOG YARD

BACK DECK

FRONT LAWN

BACK LAWN

DAY BEDS

DAY BEDS

DEVIL'S TRACK RIVER

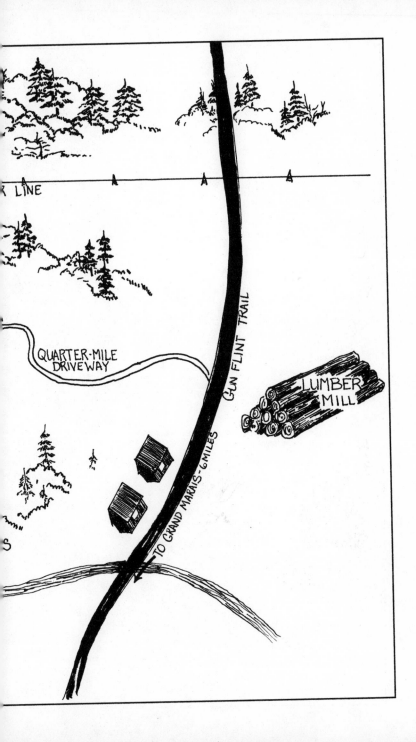

INTRODUCTION

On the night of July 8, 1988, we arrived at our new home
on Elbow Creek, north of Lake Superior. We rolled out
sleeping bags onto the living room floor and looked out at the
stars that appeared through the windows in the twilight. At
about 11 P.M., unable to sleep, I opened the sliding glass door
and stepped out onto our back deck. There, I stood listening
to the murmur of the creek, the gentle trembling of leaves, the
crack of an unseen branch in the forest, and the far-off yip of
a coyote. I smiled to myself, knowing why after so many years
I had returned to this remote country.

Some people might call this move a passage in our lives, a
rare change of lifestyles. Such a passage would have been
meaningless, however, had we not opened ourselves to the
new opportunities it offered. By moving to Elbow Creek, surrounded by forest, we had put ourselves into the home of the
bears who would make this story possible. But we had to
invite them into our lives. We had to spend time learning
about their world.

My wife, Patti, and I have come to agree that neither of us
could ever have done it alone. We certainly would not have
found the courage to reach out to the bears. Together, however, through mutual support, we found both the courage and
interest that led us to live this story for seven years.

After buying the local newspaper, Patti and I wrote columns
during the winter months about Little Bit or one of the other
bears, telling of some interesting thing we'd observed or an
adventure the bears had experienced. Most people loved the

stories and told us so in letters or when we spoke to them at the post office or grocery store. On the renewal cards we sent out, there was space for reader comments. Many mentioned how much they liked the bear stories and photos. "Keep those bear stories coming," they'd say.

Still, we could see doubt in the eyes of some of our readers. Did we really see the bears do those things or were we just pulling their leg? Did we actually go outside and sit with wild bears? Even touch them?

Nobody knew it at the time, but we were probably spending two or three hours and sometimes a lot more observing the bears each day for a period of about four months each summer. You learn a lot when you watch them constantly.

Though not trained scientists, we have read extensively and spent thousands of hours personally observing the bears and other animals about which we have written.

Of course, we did not use scientific methods in the study of these bears. They were not shot with dart guns, trapped, sedated, or monitored by radio collar. Instead, we used common sense, a gentle touch, and friendship. But scientist or not, you cannot observe an animal without changing its behavior. The mere act of being there is an intrusion, which can alter that animal's destiny.

Ultimately, we fell in love with several of the bears as we recorded their visits in a journal and with our cameras. They may have come seeking sunflower seeds to eat, but they understood us and stayed because of trust and for companionship.

Over the years, skeptics have voiced the fear that because we involved ourselves in the bears' lives, we made them lose their fear of people and become either complacent or dangerous.

"Don't you know any better?" one naysayer asked. "Bears

are dangerous. They kill people. You're asking for trouble."

Another said, "You're spoiling them. They'll think all people are nice and get themselves killed."

All of the bears we knew were good foragers and able to feed themselves without our help. Nothing we did would have rendered them unfit to live in the woods. Nor did they transfer their trust in us to others. If confronted by a stranger, even when they were on the familiar back deck or the lawn, they would invariably head for the woods. They were shy and easily frightened, and much preferred flight to any kind of conflict.

All the bears we observed were strong, powerful creatures, occasionally arguing or, even more rarely, fighting among themselves, but never aggressive or dangerous to us. It is true that people have been killed by bears, but dogs kill people too. The infrequent deaths caused by black bears have generally been isolated situations in remote areas. We think those bears were starving, were being teased, or perhaps were suffering from a chemical imbalance or mental instability. We have read about the extremely rare "crazy" bears and can understand that they might exist.

Bears cannot be lumped together in terms of personality or behavior or even intellect. They are as unique and individual as people. Most are gentle and smart. However, we would never approach a strange bear and would advise others to take the same precaution.

Ultimately, of course, we can only present you with the facts as we lived them and let you be the judge. There were many other creatures we befriended during those seven years —deer, raccoons, chipmunks, a raven, and a grouse—but what follows is primarily the story of the six seasons we spent with Little Bit and the rest of the bears.

1

RETURNING TO MINNESOTA

In the summer of 1988, Patti and I set out from Destin, Florida, to start anew in northeastern Minnesota. You'll find Destin over in the Panhandle, a little dot on the map, although you'd swear it's a bustling city from the high-rises that stretch for miles along its Gulf beaches, accommodating about 30,000 sunseeking tourists at a time.

Our destination was Grand Marais on the north shore of Lake Superior. It also shows up as a little dot on the map, but there the similarities between the two cities end. Grand Marais has one stoplight, no sand beaches, a couple of dozen tourist cabins, a few small motels, and 1,100 residents, including about twenty of my uncles, aunts, cousins, nephews, and nieces.

Grand Marais was the place my grandfather Carl Oscar put down roots after immigrating from Sweden at the turn of the century. I suppose, like most of the Swedes and Norwegians who settled there, he was reminded of the old country. It is a cold, hard place. Just when you think it's going to enjoy growth and prosperity, along comes a nasty winter or two—or maybe a summer of perpetual fog and rain—to skim off the excess and send newcomers packing. Minnesota itself is cold country, but in spring and early summer when it's 60 degrees across the rest of the state, it's apt to be only 40 or 45 in Grand Marais.

But even though my parents left during World War II for the shipyards of Superior, Wisconsin, and beyond, I have always felt a strong kinship for the place. I was only five at the time they moved, so my knowledge of Grand Marais was accumulated during visits I made while growing up in Detroit Lakes in western Minnesota.

Grand Marais was the place I caught my first brook trout in a hidden stream and trolled Lake Superior for lake trout in my father's old fishing boat. It was the place we went for cool summer vacations in August and downhill skiing in February. But mostly, it was the place at the edge of the wilderness, where there were moose and wolves and a hint of danger for the imagination to savor.

The first time I mentioned moving to Minnesota to my wife was at age forty-eight, after fifteen years in the newspaper business in Florida, when Patti and I were sitting waist-deep in our pool and enjoying a soft, balmy Florida evening. Patti, a blend of Sicilian and French-Canadian heritage, is six months my junior. From the way she cooks and cleans and moves, you could say she goes through life at a simmer.

"You're not serious," was Patti's worried reply.

But after two fall vacations among the colorful maples and aspen, energized by the brisk air, she changed her mind. When we made the decision, it was with her eager support. So, armed with enough money for a house and a long sabbatical and the determination to do some serious writing, we prepared to set off for the north country.

The moving van had come and gone when we loaded our black Lab, Ramah, and our four housecats captured from the boonies of Destin into the Jeep Cherokee, hitched up our five-by-eight-foot Adventures in Moving trailer, and headed north into the hottest day of the summer.

It was 102 degrees in Birmingham and only marginally less hot in the back of the Cherokee, where a couple of the cats appeared ready to expire. We stopped alongside the freeway and repacked to give the animals a much-improved taste of the air-conditioning. South of Nashville it was 105 degrees and felt very much like the inside of an oven.

Then, at noon on the third day, we reached Duluth. The air blowing in off the lake was a downright chilly 60. We donned our sweatshirts, opened the windows, turned off the air-conditioning for the last time, and headed up "The Shore," as Lake Superior's North Shore is called.

There had been a drought that summer in northern Minnesota, provoking a considerable fear of forest fire. You could smell the dust in the air. The streams that had been thundering merrily into Lake Superior when we'd passed through in April were now virtually dry. I wondered how the fish survived, or if they did. And I started to worry that Elbow Creek, running behind the A-frame house we were planning to buy the next morning, might have somehow dried up.

We pulled off the Gunflint Trail onto the quarter-mile driveway feeling blessed by the lovely summer weather. Carpets of white, yellow, and orange flowers filled the space between driveway and forest. Ahead, backed up to the garage, was a big, drive-it-yourself moving van. Two men, looking large and solid, came around the truck to see who it was. They were Stan Hedstrom, who owned the house but was moving to California, and Stan's brother Ed, who would become our neighbor. The men were both sandy-haired six-footers, well over two hundred pounds, with the ruddy complexions of once fair Swedish skin, burnished by sun, wind, and cold. Stan, who wore a bushy mustache, was about forty, while full-bearded Ed was a few years younger. They talked with the lilt common to that part of northern Minnesota.

The Hedstrom brothers were part of a family that had started a lumber mill seventy-five years earlier. The mill business had prospered, and now operated by a third generation, it was located on about forty acres across the Gunflint Trail from our driveway. Despite the heavy machinery and truck traffic, the mill was never intrusive. The wildlife certainly paid it no attention.

After reassuring us there was still a good supply of water in the creek, Stan showed me around the mechanical parts of the house, particularly the wood-chip-burning furnace that heated the house and whose quirky machinery would frighten us for the next couple of winters. Along with the chip burner, we got a semitrailer half full of chips. Seeing as how the chips were a by-product of the lumber mill and conveniently close by, burning them was an extremely cheap way to heat the house.

Casual talk turned to the wonders of the outdoor world around us.

"You should have seen the moose family we had around here a couple of years ago," Stan said. "They'd lie right there in front of that window, and sometimes they'd lie on the driveway so I had to drive around them. One day my wife was combing our daughter's hair and when she looked up there was a moose staring in the window at them. They're curious, you know."

For some reason, I thought of bears. I had a strong fear of them, which I attempted to implant in Patti's head as well. "Did you have any problems with bears?" I asked.

He shrugged. "We had a compost pile and they got into that."

I mentally scratched the idea of composting as the talk turned to deer hunting, then to fishing, and naturally to the weather. Conversations always turn to the weather. Nice days, windy days, snowy days, that's how you strike up a conversation in northern Minnesota. Somehow the weather is always a major factor in what you do.

The Hedstroms had just finished loading up their belongings and kindly let us move our critters and sleeping bags into the house despite the fact it wouldn't be ours until morning.

Later, lying on a hard floor atop my sleeping bag and unable to sleep, I thought about bears. At that time, and for some time after, I had definite ideas about our furry friends.

In the beginning, those ideas came from my father, who grew up in Grand Marais. He was an expert hunter and outdoorsman who felt that bears were most useful when turned into bearskin rugs. In his day, bears were routinely shot as nuisances or occasionally as targets during the annual deer hunt. This view was shared by the outdoor magazines and books I read as a boy. To quote from one, *The Complete Book of Hunting*: "when hungry, bears are recklessly intrusive and very dangerous. At all times of the year, they are unpredictable."

I remember the day when I was ten years old, sitting outside on the front steps of a house in east Duluth, and a bear came running down the driveway. It was chased by at least a dozen dogs of all sizes, who were in turn followed by a number of young men and the police. The bear was killed in a vacant woodlot across the street while I received a stern lecture on their dangers.

To such a foundation of lore attaches a fair amount of personal experience gained from four summers in that land of bear-generated traffic jams, Yellowstone Park. Nobody can spend a summer in Yellowstone, let alone four, without coming to certain conclusions about bears.

Let me say that I am well aware of the differences between grizzly bears and black bears. The grizzly is truly an awesome animal, and I've seen what it can do to cars and garbage. One evening, two friends from Canyon Hotel and I accompanied a ranger to the old garbage dump in Hayden Valley between Yellowstone Canyon and Yellowstone Lake. This dump was securely padlocked and blocked to keep tourists out. We arrived at dusk and watched as grizzly bears as big as Volkswagens went by. One huge bear stopped, looked inside the window of our car, then stood up about ten feet tall and shook our vehicle back and forth. We felt like the ingredients in a giant Mixmaster.

During my second summer in the park, I went fishing alone on a trout lake two miles off the highway, near Mt. Washburn. The lake was small, about a quarter mile in diameter. Fishing the shore, I soon found myself on the far side of the lake, away from the trail that led back to the road. I looked up and saw a black bear across the lake. At first, I paid little attention. But the bear kept moving along the shoreline until it was only a hundred yards away. I began walking, until I reached the trail leading to the road. The bear kept coming. I retreated down the trail until I was perhaps two hundred yards from the lake. The bear reached the trail and kept following. I had no fish or food, but that bear seemed very interested. I walked around a bend in the trail then broke into a run and kept it up for the entire two miles, setting some sort of a personal record in the process. I never saw that bear again, thank goodness.

And it looked like now, as an adult, I might have even scarier tales to tell. Just a week after we bought the house on Elbow Creek, Stan's wife and their two daughters were briefly trapped in a cabin on Devil's Track Lake when a bear came in through a window and started rummaging around the kitchen for dinner.

For more than a year, we lived in the north woods of Minnesota without seeing a bear on our property. We saw and befriended a number of deer and three young raccoons. We saw moose and a timber wolf in the front yard. But no bears. Judging from the "bear complaints" noted in the sheriff's report in our local newspaper, it seemed they were busy elsewhere.

Until August of 1989, when the midnight marauder made his first visit.

It was one of those hot nights when, even with the windows wide open, you find it most comfortable to sleep without covers. Even in far northeastern Minnesota, there are such nights, if only for a couple of weeks during high summer.

Behind the house, the creek was bubbling quietly on its way to Lake Superior and I was drifting off to sleep when there was a loud "thunk" made by something heavy downstairs in the dining room. We crept down to find that the dining room chair closest to the open window was turned over and our biggest cat, Einstein, was under the table with his long hair standing on end. We soon realized that the cat and something had just gone nose to nose through the screen window and that the same something had retreated after Einstein did a back flip off the chair.

We praised our terrified cat for his brave defense, closed the windows, and went back upstairs. We were still wide awake, thinking about what that something was when we heard the swish of moving bushes, then footsteps on the rocks below the window. These were heavy footsteps that caused the rocks to grate and grind beneath the enormous weight. I stiffened. Patti's hand gripped my arm.

"You hear that?" she whispered.

"Yes."

"What is it?"

" A bear, I think."

"Will it try to get in?"

" I hope not."

I pulled myself quietly from the bed and stepped to the window. Two stories down, barely illuminated by the night-light in the kitchen, was a dark shape, a large dark shape. A bear. It was near the back door of the walk-out lower level. Above that was the first-floor deck that stretched across the back of the house. The deck was supported by thick posts. The bear rose up onto its hind legs, grasped the corner post, looked up and sniffed the air.

"What's it doing?" Patti whispered.

"Getting ready to climb up onto the deck."

"Oh, my God. It's trying to get in."

The bear was large and obviously intent on finding food.

Patti sat up in bed. "What are you going to do?"

"Go downstairs to check." I did not want to go downstairs. I didn't want to go anywhere near that bear, but I said I was going, so I had to go.

I went hesitantly down the stairs into the living room, picked up a flashlight, and went to the sliding glass door that opened onto the deck. It was dark out there. A number of frightening scenarios collided inside my head. At that moment, preparing for my first inevitable confrontation, I knew I was truly afraid of bears.

Patti followed close behind me, sensing my uncertainty. "What should I do?" she asked.

"Nothing." I replied, taking a deep breath. "I'll go out and scare him off."

I flipped on the overhead light. If he'd been standing there

I'm sure I would have fainted or had a heart attack, or both. But there was nothing. I slid open the glass door enough to play the light beam over the darkened end of the deck. Still nothing but silence.

Stepping onto the deck, I kept the door open in case a quick retreat was needed. For a moment I stood tensed, listening. Then I exploded, jumping up and down on the deck, yelling and roaring in my best imitation of a demented banshee. Inside, our old Labrador joined me with enthusiastic barking.

Under the deck, at the lower level, the bear headed south, crashing over deadfalls and breaking brush. By the time we got the dog calmed down, the bear was gone. "Whoo," I exclaimed, flushed with victory. "That's one scared bear. Bet he'll be running till tomorrow morning."

He did not run till morning. The euphoria did not last. At 4:00 A.M., just as dawn was softening the darkness, I awoke. Perhaps it was the sound of the fifty-five-gallon trash barrel being overturned. Maybe it was the bird feeding station being ripped from its moorings. Whatever it was, I knew I had to go have a look around. There in the dim gray light, a very large black bear was standing brazenly on the front lawn beneath the pin cherry tree. He seemed to be studying the hummingbird feeder suspended from a limb.

I knew I should do something, but what? Go to the front door and commence screaming and yelling? The bear made up his mind before I did. Rising on hind legs, he grasped the feeder in both paws, tilted it expertly, and gulped down a quart of the sweet red nectar. By the time I reached the door, he was already ambling down the driveway. I shouted, which evoked a slow, disdainful backward glance from the well-fed visitor, and he continued on at an unhurried pace in search of other sport.

I walked outside to check the damage. The empty hummingbird feeder was still swinging, slightly above my head. That meant our marauder , standing upright, was well over six feet tall. I felt a sudden chill as I returned to the house. That night, we had learned our first lesson about bears. You can scare off a hungry bear, but it won't stay scared for long.

The weather continued warm, the windows stayed open, and a few nights after the marauder's visit, I stiffened at the sound of rocks sliding below. Oh no, I thought, the return of the marauder. But when I looked out the window, there was nothing I could see. The sounds continued. Perhaps he's just passing through, I hoped, knowing it was wishful thinking.

Patti was sleeping, so I quietly slid back into bed, waiting, listening. For several minutes, all was quiet. I could feel the tension building. Then there was noise on the back deck. Animal noise. I jumped up.

Patti sat up suddenly. "What is it?" she mumbled.

"Our bear friend is back," I said, trying to sound icy calm, like Clint Eastwood. We eased downstairs and tiptoed across the darkened living room. It was too black outside to see anything.

"I'll flip on the light and hope for the best," I whispered.

"He won't try to charge through the glass?"

"No, it's double glass plus a screen," I replied. It sounded like a safe, solid barrier, but I doubted it would even slow the old marauder. He could shatter the whole works with a slap. Sometimes you don't want to turn on a light because you don't really want to see or disturb or maybe provoke what's out there. This should have been one of those times, but someone had to do it, and I was the head of the family.

"Okay, here goes," I announced, steeling myself. My hand kept on shaking.

The light flipped on and we stood in silence. "Oh, my God," was all I could manage.

A huge smile brightened Patti's face. "Aren't they just the cutest things you've ever *seen*."

Two cub bears, looking very much like furry little puppies, were standing on their hind legs, gobbling sunflower seeds from the bench that surrounded the deck. They were about three feet tall head to toe and were not bothered one bit by the light.

"Oh, they're so hungry. Can't we just let them have the seeds?" Patti asked.

"If we don't chase them off, really scare them, they'll be back every night. Little bears grow up to become big bears. Besides, mama bear is around somewhere and if there's one thing we don't need, it's an angry mother bear around here."

My speech fell on deaf ears. Patti was oohing over the cubs. Meanwhile, an idea took root in my brain. I went to the closet and returned with the shotgun.

"Oh no, you wouldn't."

"Of course not. But I'm gonna scare them good." I loaded a shell into the chamber. "Okay now, we'll open the sliding door just enough to get the barrel out and I'll aim up over their heads. When this thing goes off, you're gonna see bears flying in all directions." I loaded a second shell in the magazine, in case the explosion triggered a charge. This may sound ridiculous, but at the time even little bears frightened me.

"Okay now, here goes." I slid open the door and poked the barrel through. The cubs were only eight feet from the door, but undisturbed. The shotgun roared. Ka-boom!

Outside, the scene remained unchanged. One cub turned his head lazily to see what the noise was about. The other didn't even bother, just kept sucking up seeds like a vacuum cleaner. I couldn't believe it. Neither could Patti. So I took what seemed a logical next step, sliding open the door and doing my banshee routine. That caught their attention, and

Winter at the house on Elbow Creek.

they scampered across the deck and down the stairs to join their mother, who was waiting below.

Surprisingly, neither the marauder nor the pair of cubs returned that fall. Nor did any other bears. The leaves turned gold and fluttered down, carpeting the ground. The days became shorter, colder. One October morning, we woke up to a white world and the start of a long winter that would bring 138 inches of snowfall.

Time passed quickly. In October, we took over the ownership of the local weekly newspaper, *The Cook County News Herald*, and went back to work. During those first several months, we spent long hours learning the ropes, fine-tuning the paper, meeting people. And before we even had time to get into the rhythm of winter, the April thaw was upon us.

The spring of 1990 was sudden and short. One minute we

were marveling at Percy, our resident partridge, drumming from atop a snowdrift in his attempt to meet a local female partridge; the next we were seeing crocuses in bloom and catkins on the aspens. The deer came back in the spring, look-ing gaunt and tired from doing battle all winter with deep snow and wolves, and we put out a pile of corn to help them on their way.

One day in late May, Patti finished her work at the office and went home early. She was excited and out of breath when she called. "You'll never believe it," she gasped into the phone. "Mama bear and her two cubs were at the corn pile when I drove in. They ran away but came right back. They're out there now."

"That's unreal," I replied, not quite sure how to take the news.

Unreal or not, it marked the beginning of a time we would always remember—as our summers with the bears.

The bear family took up residence. First, we'd see them at the corn pile, then we'd hear the cubs scampering up trees in the dark. They were never far away. I wanted to start on the garden, but the fear of getting between mother and cubs was a deterrent. We were also worried that our old Labrador, Ramah, would try to chase the cubs and end up face to face with you know who.

After a few edgy days, I talked with Patti. "The bears are fun to watch," I said, "but they worry me. Somehow we need to scare them off."

She nodded, though I knew she was disappointed. "So how are we going to chase them away?" she asked.

I thought about the problem and came up with a primitive solution. "Throw rocks and yell?" I suggested. But I soon learned that bears are quickly able to assess the range of a rock thrower and stay just beyond it. No rock came within ten feet of a bear. Also after a half-dozen throws, my arm felt as if it had been separated from my shoulder. "So much for throwing rocks and yelling," I said. We gave up for the evening.

Day two began with the bears lolling on the front yard. Patti went out the door to frighten them away. Mama bear took one look and charged, sending Patti racing for the door. She came inside, gasping for breath. "Did you see that? She tried to get me."

At that time, we knew nothing about the false charges that bears will sometimes make. They puff and blow and click their teeth and charge forward a few feet, then stop. It was an unnerving experience and sealed Patti's conviction that somehow the bears must go. That evening we tried chasing them with the Jeep. Safer for us, but no more effective. The cubs climbed the trees and mother bear hid just out of sight until we backed away. Then the family reunited.

Next day, a neighbor told us about the sure-fire balloon remedy. This consisted of filling balloons with an ammonia-and-water mix, then coating them with honey and hanging them from branches within reach of the bears. She said she was trying the balloon remedy that very evening. A great idea, I thought. It would lure the bears, then when they popped the balloons, they'd get a bitter surprise. By dusk, we'd filled and coated eight balloons and left them hanging festively along the driveway. I could hardly wait for morning.

When Patti got up and looked out, she counted nine balloons scattered along the driveway. "Wait a second," she said. "We only put out eight."

The bears had not only licked the honey off every balloon without puncturing any, but they had also carried one of our neighbor's balloons over to our house, a distance of a half mile.

That day, I called the local office of the Department of

Natural Resources and talked to Wildlife Supervisor Bill Peterson, who wrote an occasional column for the newspaper. He chuckled over the story of the balloons.

"Well," he said slowly, "you won't likely get rid of them if there's anything to eat around. Once you've eliminated that, you might try a slingshot. That sometimes does the trick."

We went home that afternoon with a slingshot from the Lake Superior Trading Post. Sure enough, I managed to hit mama bear about three times in the rump during the course of the evening. The first mosquito hatch of the season was under way that evening as well, and I collected several dozen itchy bites for my efforts before remembering to douse myself in Off. But the bears did leave. They didn't return for a day, then two days, then three. After a week, we were optimistic. "I think they're gone," I said. "I think we've discouraged them."

Indeed, since the bear family had left, the deer had returned. Several were grazing on our newly sprouted grass each evening, romping and chasing each other in their enthusiasm. After a second week, we declared victory. We'd almost forgotten the bears had ever been there. The garden was planted and the radishes were already peeking through the rocky soil.

And then, one week later, Little Bit came down the driveway and into our lives.

2

LITTLE BIT ARRIVES

The cicadas were singing on that sunny, high-summer afternoon when Little Bit made her way along the narrow grassy strip between the gravel driveway and the dense forest, strolling like a little hobo with no schedules to keep.

"Better come and have a look," I called to Patti, who was in the kitchen fixing iced tea. She came into the dining room at a quick step and followed my eyes out the front window.

"Oh, he's just a poor little orphan," she exclaimed as the cub moved unerringly toward the sunflower seed pan we'd put out on a stump for the birds. "Can we just let him have a little something to eat?" She pleaded, knowing full well we had worked all spring trying to get the bears to move elsewhere.

I was still afraid of bears, even the small fry, but I judged this little scavenger to be no larger than half the size of Ramah and figured I could deal with that. "I suppose it's okay," I finally replied. By then, the little bear had already discovered the sunflower seeds and needed no further invitation.

Patti, a city girl from Rochester, New York, was always the one in her family who brought the stray dogs home from school. She had never met an animal she didn't like, and now she was looking to include bears on her list. "I'm going out to see if he has enough seeds," she announced, hurrying toward the front door. The little orphan didn't know it yet, but he was about to be welcomed into the Becklund family.

"You be careful now, in case his mother is lurking over in the woods," I admonished. My words never even slowed her down. She stepped outside and the cub retreated to the pin cherry tree, where he stood upright, holding the trunk in case escape became necessary.

For two or three minutes, Patti watched the bear and he watched her. Then, seeing something that convinced him she meant no harm, the cub dropped onto all fours and nervously edged back toward the pan of tasty seeds.

A yearling, he weighed no more than twenty-five or thirty pounds but seemed to be in good condition, with a short, shiny coat of black fur that had grown in as the old winter coat was shed.

Still standing at the dining room window, I watched as Patti remained seated on the grass, talking quietly to the cub. She has a way with animals, and her manner invoked trust in the little bear. Soon, he was eating cautiously just four feet from where she sat cross-legged in the grass. The two sat that way, sharing a shady place on the lawn, for nearly a half hour until the ample mound of seeds had vanished. When Patti eased to her feet, the cub retreated only halfway to the pin cherry tree, then returned to search the grass around the pan for any stray seeds.

"Wow!" Patti said happily as she came in the door. "Did you see that? We've got a little female bear cub out there. I think she'll come right up to me. Isn't she just beautiful?" She could hardly contain her excitement.

She set out more seeds in the pan and sat down again on the grass, where she watched as the bear came back and resumed eating. By now, however, the blood-thirsty Minnesota mosquitoes had descended. The cub paid them no heed, but Patti was starting to swat and shoo. She retreated inside.

"Isn't she a perfect little bear?" Patti called to me. "A little miniature of an adult bear! I think we should call her Little something. How about Little Bit?" Unbeknownst to us at the time was that the cub had officially been adopted.

For the next two days, for as much as an hour each day, the familiarizing process continued. Patti would watch for the cub, spritz herself from head to toe with Deep Woods Off and go outside. Eventually the two would be sitting directly across the seed pan from each other.

Patti would come in from each encounter thrilled at the progress she and Little Bit were making. "I touched her today," she related excitedly, "and she never even retreated. She just lies there in front of me and looks at me like she's trying to fig-ure me out."

On the third day, we decided to try to move Little Bit from the front yard to the back deck. My truck coming and going on the dusty driveway frightened her. Then too, the small group of deer we'd collected loved to run and chase each other around the front lawn and garden area every morning and evening. With the cub in back, they'd be more likely to stay around. Moving her there was surprisingly simple: where her seed pan went, so went Little Bit. Patti called to her to come along and she did, taking up residence on what was to become her own deck, the future setting for many of our bear adven-tures.

The back deck was thirty-two feet long overall and eight feet wide along half its length outside the sliding glass door. It was wider, about fourteen feet, on the other end nearest the steps that led down half a level to a smaller deck. Because the

Patti and Little Bit get acquainted.

house had a walk-out basement, the deck hovered one story off the ground and stood on posts, overlooking Elbow Creek a hundred feet away. The creek flowed into Devil's Track River, then ran down into Lake Superior six miles away.

The deck was surrounded by a built-in bench seat with back rest, topped by a two-by-six-inch railing. Because the deck drew fewer mosquitoes than the grass, we often ate lunch outdoors at a wrought-iron table set up in the wider area. The day we moved Little Bit to the back was a sunny one. When we went out that day for lunch, Little Bit quickly joined us. She found my leather moccasin much more tasty than anything else she might have eaten, and I had to dissuade her from taking it, foot and all. But she was extremely gentle, and Patti was soon ruffling her coat as they sat outside together.

We had always put out seeds along the top of the railing for the birds that came along, but now that most of our feathered friends were off raising young, Little Bit ate the lion's share—or, more accurately, the bear's share.

We had not settled into a routine with her or even gotten accustomed to seeing her on the deck when we were treated to a shock later in the week. Patti looked out and I suddenly heard her say, "Oh my gosh, what's happened to you? Have you been in a fight? Are you sick?" She hurried across the living room, and I glanced up to see the mangiest, most moth-eaten cub you could ever imagine. We both thought something terrible had happened to our happy, well-fed yearling.

When Patti opened the door, the cub flew across the deck and down the stairs. It still hadn't occurred to us that this was a stranger until at the bottom of the steps, the scrawny cub literally ran into Little Bit. Both fled in opposite directions and ended up in adjacent trees, where they took the measure of each other.

When Little Bit had taken up residence, we had picked up a booklet about black bears to help us understand their behavior. Thus we already knew that mother bears abandoned their cubs in June of their second summer. They did this before mating, which meant they had cubs every other spring. The two cubs that had just sent themselves into trees weren't exactly orphans but had been recently set adrift by their mothers. We wondered if the newcomer was one of the cubs we had recently chased away.

The booklet also said that cubs fear larger bears more than anything else because adult bears sometimes injure or even kill cubs. Each cub obviously thought the other was larger and constituted a threat, so up the trees they'd sped. Now we had two cubs, each one huffing and puffing to scare the other and each wishing its mother was still around for protection.

They finally came down and departed in separate direc-

Skinny's first portrait.

tions, but a while later they returned together, apparently set on becoming friends. I shook my head, thinking that I should draw the line at one cub. But before I finished pondering, Patti had already named the cowlick-harboring newcomer "Skinny," and I knew the decision to extend our welcome had been made without me.

Skinny was a boy bear and as different in many ways from Little Bit as night and day.

The first thing we noticed was that he was shy and absolutely would not look us in the eye. He would look up, down, sideways, and backward, anywhere except at us. Perhaps the idea was that if he didn't look at you, you weren't really there. Or maybe you wouldn't see him. We didn't know it yet, but this was a trait most young bears exhibit. Even adults will seldom make eye contact with a stranger. Little Bit, with her direct eye contact from day one, was certainly the exception.

As yearlings, whenever the cubs scented danger they went scrambling into the nearest tree, an old white spruce next to the deck. The spruce rose about twenty-five feet to a jagged top that had been sheared by lightning. The lowest ten feet were without branches, but above that branches stuck out like a hundred porcupine quills. Only the top ones carried needles; the rest had been gobbled up by the spruce budworms during the late eighties.

But if to our eyes the tree looked weary and near death, the cubs saw it as a safe haven. When in doubt as to their where-abouts, we could look up in the cradling branches of the old spruce and would be likely to find a cub looking back down.

During August of that first summer, Little Bit and Skinny became inseparable. And thanks to Patti's ever-heaping sun-flower seed bowls, they put on weight rapidly and began to look like a pair of roly-poly fur balls. Skinny's tangled mat of hair even grew silky.

I was amazed at the quantity of seeds they were consuming. Every time I looked out, they were lying on the deck, munching happily. The fifty-pound bags were disappearing at a rate that was threatening our budget. I was getting worried.

"Don't they seem to be eating an awful lot?" I asked Patti. "They must spend eight hours a day at those seed bowls."

"I suppose they need more food to get ready for hibernation," she said with a shrug.

Then one day, I went out on the deck and the two yearlings jumped up from their bowls and ran off into the woods. I couldn't understand why they'd do that when normally they would hardly raise their heads. It almost seemed like they didn't know us. Suddenly, a lightbulb went on in my brain. These bears weren't Skinny and Little Bit but *another* pair they had befriended.

Two nights later, we knew the truth. As dusk fell, Little Bit and Skinny wandered out to the side yard and were joined by three other juveniles. Now we had five, Little Bit and four others. Every one of those four was a male, as we could easily see when in the evening, they would gather in the side yard behind the garage for play sessions. They wrestled, chased each other, stood on their hind legs boxing, and rolled around contentedly.

At first, Skinny was reluctant to enter in. He seemed to have been a lone cub, for he didn't readily understand the concept of play. But the others kept after him, cuffing him playfully and running away, until Skinny finally picked it up.

By September 1, the opening of bear hunting season, we had accumulated nine juveniles around the house. Though only in their second summer, they seemed to understand that they were safe here, and that led us to call our place ever after "The Sanctuary." Once we'd thought of the name, we decided

Little Bit and friends on the back lawn.

that our home would be a sanctuary for all birds and animals that found their way there. And over the years, as the newspaper grew and prospered, even the sunflower seed expenses became tolerable.

One evening that first week of September, a huge bear whose fur nearly swept the ground lumbered down the driveway toward the house. The bear had a large white chest blaze, which made us certain we'd never seen it before. The young bears stopped in their play to watch the big bear's advance. We expected them to flee in all directions within seconds. But then Little Bit walked confidently out to meet the newcomer. If she'd been a dog, she would have wagged her tail. The two met in the front yard, then proceeded together to where the other bears were waiting. Soon, the big bear was lying on its back, legs outspread, allowing the youngsters to climb all over it. We called it Grandfather bear, but Grandmother might have been appropriate. We were never able to figure out its gender.

The scene was and still is a mystery to us. Usually, an adult bear will chase a cub. Bigger bears' aggression is a major cause of death among cubs. Yet these young bears, less than a quarter of the big bear's size, played with him until it was nearly dark. Others we talked to were mystified as well. There is much about bear behavior that is still unknown, even to the experts who have devoted their lives to its study.

Another evening, a second adult bear made an appearance. Little Bit was sitting with Patti on the back deck and appeared to be unconcerned at the advance of the adult. Still new to the ways of bears, Patti thought the adult might constitute a threat to the yearling, so she got up, picked up the outdoor broom, and banged it on the floor. The bear stopped and looked. Patti yelled and advanced with Little Bit right on her heels. The bear backed up two steps. Patti banged the broom handle again. Finally, the bear got the message. It turned and looked back over its shoulder as it walked slowly away. Patti later commented on how sad the bear looked.

To make sure the bear continued on its way, she walked out on the lawn. Within a few seconds, she felt a tug on her pantleg, then a paw pulling on her ankle. Startled, she looked down to see Little Bit tugging against her leg. Understanding took only a moment. She was on a patch of grass where the yearlings rolled and tumbled. Since she had walked out to the playground, Little Bit thought she wanted to play.

By mid-September our pack of juveniles started to dwindle. We didn't know it at the time, but they were already going off to hibernate. We had thought they would hibernate in late October or early November, when the snows came. But in northeastern Minnesota bears usually start hibernating much earlier, during the last two weeks of September or very early October.

Occasionally, a young bear will delay denning, either because of lack of food or the discovery of a good source of food, until late in the season. Skinny was a good example. Having finally found plenty of food, he was reluctant to leave. Night after night, he would appear and sit alone out on the deck. One night, during the season's first snowfall, Skinny, having resumed his usual post, became covered in snow like a huge rock. Almost asleep on his feet at the time, he didn't move for a couple of hours. When we looked up to see him peering through the glass door, he was wearing snow like a lacy white veil across his ears.

When Skinny finally left, well into October and long after Little Bit had gone, early winter set in and we were left with memories of a strange and exceptional summer. With the melting of that first snow, we could still see a narrow path cut into the grass of the back and side yard. The path was only a

One of the yearlings at the end of our first summer
with the bears.

few inches wide and went down to bare dirt. Despite having a
spacious yard to travel across, all the bears had used this same
little path. We wondered why. We had seen a lot of bears and
thought we had learned a great deal about them, but we were

only starting to learn. We had barely dipped our toes into the world of bears. Understanding would come much later.

By late April of the following year, bears began to be sighted along the North Shore, and people started asking if our friends had returned. We'd seen no sign of them, but we weren't worried. We figured they had a long way to travel and knew that bears don't start the journey until they are fully alert. Also, Elbow Creek was a barrier in the spring, at least for smaller bears.

It was mid-May when Skinny finally came back. At least we thought it was Skinny. Young bears change a lot from fall to early spring. They lose up to a third of their weight. They look gangly, and their fur is straggly, as they shed their heavy winter coats. So when Skinny arrived, it was only by his actions that we recognized him.

"Wait a minute," Patti said, one morning, "that bear stands up to look inside the house, just like Skinny did." After you watch any bear for a while, you notice its unique way of doing things. Thus, after a couple of days of thinking how much the moth-eaten young bear resembled Skinny, we were sure it was indeed he. He was larger than a year earlier, but just about as frazzled as he had been when we first saw him.

Every day thereafter, we worried about Little Bit. Had she been shot by a hunter the previous fall? Had she succumbed to the ravages of a hard winter? Had she simply set off in another direction after awakening from six months of sleep? Had she been hurt on her way to our house in the spring? Every time we heard a gunshot, we thought the worst.

Our fears persisted until Memorial Day, when late in the morning Little Bit casually walked up on the deck with Skinny close behind. We recognized her immediately. She looked directly at Patti as if to say, "Of course I'm here. What did you expect?" Thin but not quite gaunt, she was about two or three inches shorter than Skinny. She sat down, legs splayed out as usual, and commenced eating seeds as though she'd been away only a day or two.

That time of year, Elbow Creek was a rumbling presence in our lives. It ran below our place, joined with Devil's Track River, then continued down through a deep canyon to Lake Superior. Most of the summer, it was a pleasantly bubbling and gurgling trout stream about ten or fifteen feet wide, but in the spring, during the snow melt and runoff, the creek came alive. It drained about a hundred square miles of wilderness swamps and lakes, so the water ran fast and deep when the snow melted or heavy rains fell.

One day in late May, just after Little Bit returned, we saw a strange mother bear and her two cubs passing through. Bears often did this. We'd see them crossing the driveway toward the river, wonder who they were, then never see them again. They were simply traveling, using the river as a conduit to go someplace else. Female bears sometimes wander over home territories of five or ten square miles. Males take trips of fifty miles or more. The mother bear had passed through awhile earlier, and we had gone out back to clear some brush for a better view of the creek from our back deck.

Suddenly a high-pitched squalling could be heard over the roar of the water.

"Did you hear that?" Patti asked. We stood up to locate the sound, then realized it was a cub being swept downstream in the creek, and it was bawling for help. Fortunately, help wasn't far behind. Before the yearling cub floated out of sight around the bend, his mother came racing downstream along the bank, breaking brush as she ran. She caught up with the screaming cub about two hundred yards downstream and leaped into the water. We were unable to get a clear view, but soon she had hauled the frightened cub out of the creek and shooed it ahead of her along the streambed.

We stood there watching as mother and cub came back upstream and passed us without even looking our way. Once they were out of sight, we could hear the noise of another cub sliding down a tree as the trio was reunited. The mother and cubs went on their way, and we never saw them again. However, we learned from the episode that Elbow Creek was a major danger in the spring, especially to a mother with new cubs. It was also one of the reasons the bears didn't arrive at our house some years until the first of June.

In his third summer, Skinny changed rapidly. Having learned to enjoy the company of other bears his age, he now began to seek them out. Every week or so, he would leave by himself and go off for a period of three or four days, always returning with a new juvenile friend. We called these adventures "Skinny's walkabouts." It was as if he had appointed himself Pied Piper of the bear world and was determined to share his largesse with others.

We'd be sitting outside on the deck and here would come Skinny with a new friend. He'd walk directly up the steps and sit down to eat from the seed box, leaving his new friend standing down below, wondering what to do. Strange bears, especially juveniles and cubs, do not simply walk up to humans. To his friends, Skinny was doing the unthinkable.

Another thing that had changed about Skinny was that he was now making eye contact with us. Before, he would come up on the deck but never acknowledge us with his eyes. Now that he knew us, he would look directly at us, which confused his friends even more.

By mid-summer, Skinny had brought home half a dozen

young male bears. Those that stayed around got named. There was Scar, a gentle bear named for the scar that ran from above his right eye to his temple. Sarge got his name because he had three white stripes on his chest. Toby liked to eat corn and sometimes hung out with Sarge. Irving was a solitary bear who mostly stayed up by the garden. The other bears didn't like him because he snapped at them when they came near his corn pile.

Skinny was now a tall and leggy bear who would fill out to become a large male. He had already emerged as the natural leader of the juvenile boys around the house, maybe because of his seniority and his familiarity with the house and us.

One day, Patti, my younger son, Tom, from Minneapolis, and I were outside on the deck when Skinny returned from his

Skinny grew tall and lanky.

latest walkabout. Tom was twenty-nine years old at the time. He had graduated from college, tried his hand as a theater lighting director with several road versions of Broadway hits, and now was working in home health care. He was a city kid who liked to come up and visit us in the woods. He looked burly enough to wrestle a bear, but was really quite easygoing.

As the bear climbed the steps to the deck, Tom sucked in his breath suddenly. He'd never been outside with bears around. "Oh oh," he said quietly. Patti and I immediately recognized Skinny, but not the bear with him. Skinny went straight to the sunflower seeds. The other bear averted its eyes and waited at the top of the stairs, hoping for a clue of some kind. It was still waiting when Little Bit arrived several minutes later. Eventually, confused, it went up a tree. Little Bit marched up to Skinny as if to say, "What's going on?" They sniffed each other and touched noses, then each sat down to eat, ignoring Skinny's friend in the tree.

As for Tom, just being out there with the bears was thrill enough for one day. He couldn't wait to get back to the city, eager to tell about the bears he'd met.

As Skinny was taking on more male characteristics, Little Bit was becoming a young lady. As she changed physically, her behavior also began to change in ways we did not expect. She would not come up on the deck with anybody but Skinny. She would not join the males in the evening for roughhouse sessions. When they played, she came up and sat on the deck with us. She preferred taking sunflower seeds and nuts from Patti's hand instead of from the box. Sometimes Patti could not even feel the seeds being removed. Little Bit's touch was as gentle as a butterfly.

Mostly Little Bit and Skinny just hung out together. I suppose you could say he was her first love.

At that time, Little Bit did not exactly dominate the

Becklund bear scene. She did, however, bring out the best side of Skinny, who was just starting to show signs of becoming a bit of a hooligan when he was around the boys. Once, they pulled several siding boards off the back of the garage. He had also started ripping insulation off the outside basement wall. These were obviously traits that did not endear him to his hosts. I'm sure he thought the moves would help him gain access to the house, whence his sunflower seeds came. But when Little Bit batted her long eyelashes (yes, she had them) Skinny would obediently follow her around all day, generally staying out of trouble.

One day in late afternoon, we were standing on the driveway. Three of the young males were wandering across the side yard. They appeared to be making for the well-shaded grassy

Little Bit and Skinny, early in their third summer.

area near the garden, where we sometimes put corn. The area had an elevation about twenty feet higher than the surrounding terrain, so the view was excellent.

We weren't paying close attention because the bears were now familiar to us, but suddenly, the male bears heard something coming from the direction of the garden. One peeled off and fled immediately, while the other two hesitated, standing up on their hind legs to get a better view. Out onto the lawn charged a huffing, puffing bear. The juveniles—Scar, Sarge, and Toby—ran for the woods and the safety of tall trees. But the attacker was close behind, and went up a tree right behind the unlucky Toby. Together, the two bears literally raced up the tree some seventy-five feet to the top. Only then did the pursuer back off down the tree a few feet.

Meanwhile, Patti and I had retreated toward the house. "What's going on?" she asked.

I shook my head, "I don't have a clue."

In the excitement, Scar somehow managed to slip away, but the aggressive bear still had two treed bears, Sarge and Toby. He stood beneath the tall poplars, waiting and watching. As soon as one of the males tried to come down, the bear would race to the tree and climb rapidly, driving the bear back up. We were about fifty yards away, standing quietly and watching the attack. Again and again, the aggressive bear drove the juveniles back up the trees. He didn't seem to be any larger than the young males, who probably weighed close to 150 to 175 pounds by then. But he had them totally defeated. They clung to those trees as if their lives were in peril, and they probably were.

"I think that may be one of those rare crazy bears we've been reading about," Patti said. "You know, the one in a million that will attack people or anything without warning. We're just lucky he didn't come for us instead of the bears. I can't climb a tree as fast as they can."

"You're probably right," I said. "Maybe we should try scaring him off so the boys can escape." I tried the slingshot, but couldn't hit the well-camouflaged bear. Between rushes, he seemed to melt into the bushes.

"Okay, let's try the Jeep," I said. Patti looked at me doubtfully. At that time, both of us felt there was a good chance the Jeep would be attacked. We expected the bear to jump out at us at any moment. I put the vehicle in four-wheel drive and we pushed through the brush toward the scene of action. Finally, the strange bear broke and ran. I blasted on the horn for good measure.

We made a short loop and came out by the garden, stopping to open the windows to hear what was happening. We expected to hear big bears sliding down poplar trees. Instead, we heard the distinctive call of a first-year cub directly overhead in the branches of a huge spruce. I looked up and spotted two of them. Their cries were similar in pitch and intensity to the "wa-wa" of a Siamese cat.

"Oh, my gosh. You don't suppose." Patti stopped. "Our crazy bear is a mother bear protecting her cubs."

"If that's the case, she is one fierce mother," I said in awe of the small female we would continue to refer to as Crazy Bear.

Driving back across the lawn, we could hear Sarge and Toby sliding down to make their escape. They had learned something about mother bears. Next time, they'd never hesitate, they'd just run away.

Despite the rare bear-against-bear attacks we observed, such as this one by the supposedly Crazy Bear, it became obvious over the years that almost all bears preferred to bluff, posture, and threaten than to actually fight. After all, these are big, powerful animals. Somebody could get hurt.

Juveniles at the seed box.

Some of this posturing would occur around food. The early seed tray we used, soon bent and destroyed, was replaced by a sturdy, rough-hewn box we had found on one of our forest exploration trips. The box was about two feet square and six inches deep. It would hold thirty to forty pounds of seeds and was just big enough for one hungry cub to climb inside.

Inevitably, as they grew larger, each of the juvenile males wanted to control the seed box. First, they'd clamp a big paw on it and try to pull it toward them. Then would come the curious braying sound we call "crooning." This is hard to describe in words, but goes like this: "Waaaaa-wah-wah-wah"—a staccato burst in a single, high-pitched note. You get three male bears all crooning in different notes, and it sounds like a chorus warming up. They are apt to go on for several minutes at varying intensities and pitches to show their determination to dominate.

Patti and I have heard bears "croon" over food hundreds of times, sometimes with jaws open or even teeth snapping, but we've rarely seen any physical violence result from it unless one bear is considerably larger or more aggressive and another gives way, in which case a brief chase might ensue.

Late August of that summer was hot. Not just warm, but a real old-fashioned scorcher. Until Labor Day, temperatures reached into the nineties. We had planned to go to the state fair that year but changed our minds when we saw the Twin Cities were roasting. Instead, we stayed home with our gang of juvenile bears and enjoyed thoughts of hunters sweating in their tree stands.

There was a small pool in Elbow Creek, right below the house, where we could look out and watch as the bears submerged themselves in the cool water. They enjoyed that, but they mostly laid around in the shade, doing as little as possible. Their heavy winter fur had grown in thick and long, capturing whatever heat they generated.

Little Bit would come and sit with us on the deck when the others wrestled on the lawn. She was hot, panting, and uncomfortable.

"I've got something you might like, Little Bit," Patti said to

the bear. She went in, opened a small can of Carnation condensed milk, and mixed it with a gallon of ice-cold water. Well,
you would have thought that bear had died and gone to heav-
en. She sucked up the milk in about thirty seconds flat and
turned back to Patti as if to say, "Thanks for the treat."
Thereafter, on special occasions, we knew what she enjoyed
best of all.

Little Bit, like all bears, often rubbed her back against the
bench seats that circled the deck. We read they do it to leave
their mark, but to us it seemed more a case of having an itchy
back than of making a conscious effort. She also started to rub
up against Patti, as if to tell her she wanted attention. At this
point, Patti would put a few nuts on the deck or the bench
seat, only to have Little Bit ignore them and nuzzle to be
hand-fed. I guess she was becoming what one might call a
"touching" bear, or maybe a spoiled brat.

The last couple of weeks before hibernation were always the
hardest for the bears. Besides being hunted, they were terribly
hungry and the food supply was drying up. Often, the experts
say, a bear will lose some weight during that period of time.
So we kept a good supply of corn and seeds available in early
September to keep the boys from wandering into trouble with
the hunters.

Around Labor Day, another visitor showed up determined
to share the food. Night had fallen when we heard something
on the deck. Patti stepped out with her flashlight. There were
no bears or raccoons around, so she went over to the darkened end for a look at the lower level. That's when she missed
stepping on newcomer Mr. Pepe Le Pew by about an inch. The
skunk stood close to her foot when she shined the light down,
but for some reason, he didn't spray her.

Little Bit wasn't so lucky. She returned the next day

Portrait of a Young Lady.

smelling exactly like Pepe, then looked forlornly through the living room window when we wouldn't come out and sit with her. Pepe was at our house for about a week, then was never seen again. Little Bit gave us the "vapors" for a couple of days before the smell dissipated.

Believe it or not, bears normally smell quite neutral or at least reflect their surroundings. Little Bit often smelled of pine. We laughed and called her our furry Christmas tree. Only then, when she ran into Mr. Le Pew, did she ever smell bad.

3

LAND OF TWO CLIMATES, BLUEBERRIES AND BEARS

In Minnesota, we lived in a rural area of Cook County called Maple Hill. Six miles north of Grand Marais, and a thousand feet higher in altitude, it occupied land that had been settled by hardy Swedes and Norwegians who felt at home in the rolling hills and cool climate. They tried their hand at farming and managed to harvest potatoes, rutabagas, and other root crops in the rocky soil, but little else. With a growing season of less that ninety days, they were lucky to cut a crop of hay for the horses and cows. Corn was too slow.

Today, 88 percent of Cook County's 3,000 square miles is owned by federal, state, and local governments. There are about 4,000 residents, the smallest population of any county in the state. Though not conducive to farming and unable to sustain even one full-time agricultural operation, the region

supports an abundant crop of wildlife: moose, bear, deer, timber wolves, coyotes, beaver, fisher, marten, bobcat, lynx,
otters, and even an occasional mountain lion. It may not be
stretching the truth to say there are more bears in the county
than people.

The area is unique in Minnesota because it has two climates. Along Lake Superior, the lake waters keep the summers cold and the winters relatively moderate. Away from the
lake and higher up, where we lived, it was ten or twenty
degrees warmer in the summer and that much colder in the
winter. We always got a lot more snow up there, too. Because
of the two climates, our deer herd actually migrated down to
the shore of Lake Superior in winter and back to the high-
lands in spring. Following the various deer herds down to the
lake during the winter, wolves and coyotes would often prowl
the ice along the shore in hopes of picking off an unwary deer.
In the spring, melting would occur much earlier along the
shoreline than inland. So, while people were reporting sleepy-
looking bears wandering near the lake, bears a few miles away
were still snoozing happily under three feet of snow.

The spring of 1992 was the first time Patti and I really
awaited the return of our bear friends with excitement. We
actually expected them to come back, especially Skinny and
Little Bit.

By now, word that we had a group of bears visiting us had
spread around (it doesn't take long) and some of the residents
were concerned. That year in early May, a lady who lived a
couple of miles away complained to us that one of "our" bears
had already been by to destroy her bird feeder. We tried to
explain that these bears were wild, free to come and go, and
that there were many other bears out there besides the few
that we knew. She remained skeptical.

We always hoped that all the bears we had named and

befriended would return in the spring. That spring it actually happened. They all survived the fall bear hunt and the winter hibernation to return to us, the first and only time this ever occurred in the years we lived on Elbow Creek. Bears in zoos live to be twenty or twenty-five years of age, but bears in the wild rarely reach the age of seven or eight because of the many dangers they face, primarily people with guns.

The bears we knew were starting their fourth summer, now as three-year-olds. The boys, all except Skinny, came back about the middle of May—Scar, Toby, Sarge, and W.H. They were joined by a handsome male we called Pretty Boy. We could recognize him easily by his light-colored muzzle.

One day, a few weeks later, I was coming up the back steps. Having already gotten acquainted, I took casual notice of him resting on the lawn.

"Pretty Boy. How ya doing, old fellow?" He got up and started backing away. I stopped to watch his unusual behavior. He kept backing away until he reached the bushes at the edge of the woods, a distance of well over a hundred feet. I shook my head and went inside, where I told Patti of his strange retreat.

That evening, a couple of the boys were wrestling and playing on the lawn, as usual. Pretty Boy was lying down near them but not participating. When he saw us approaching, he again got up and started to walk backwards, keeping his eyes fixed on us the entire time. "There, that's what I was trying to explain," I said. The bear retreated deep into the forest, leaving us wondering what was going on.

Pretty Boy was back on the lawn the following day, where he repeated his odd behavior. Finally, a couple of days later, when we looked out and saw him, he was wrestling and playing with Sarge, just as though everything was again normal. I was ready to turn away and to write off his strange retreats as just another unexplained bear oddity, when Patti tugged on my arm, "Look. He's bleeding. I'm sure that's blood running down his coat."

Her eyes are better than mine, so it took me a while longer to spot it. There was definitely something running from high on his left hip and it certainly looked red. Continuing to watch him, we soon identified what looked like a bullet hole. Next day, we were able to get a better look at what was almost certainly a bullet hole with a scab over it and a bit of crusty blackened blood on his fur. He'd obviously been off somewhere, gotten himself shot as he was running away, then came back to us to recuperate. He seemed to be getting along well until he started wrestling. The activity broke open the wound again.

As for his strange backing-up retreat, Pretty Boy was simply trying to avoid being shot. Since he had been wounded while running away, he was determined to avoid giving anyone the same target. By backing away, he was simply protecting his injured hip as best he could. The wound repeatedly crusted over and broke open for two or three weeks before healing permanently. He was never entirely comfortable in our company again.

Little Bit came back the last week in May in good condition, very nearly as large and heavy as her male juvenile acquaintances. We had half expected her to be bringing a cub along—since she and Skinny had seemingly mated the previous summer right on our front lawn, and more than once—but there was no cub.

Skinny arrived shortly after Little Bit, to complete the cast of characters. He was becoming quite large and more insistent on getting his own way. I made a move to get up to go inside, and he spun around with his paw out and cuffed my shirt, barely missing my side. I'm sure this was a natural defensive

Little Bit at Patti's side.

action, but thereafter I moved more deliberately around him. He trotted after Patti, however, like a large black puppy.

Although he was still gentle and almost courtly to Little Bit, Skinny started to put a strain on his relations with me in other ways as well. One night, we were awakened by thudding and crashing on the lower deck. We went down to find Skinny trying to pull apart the basement door.

We began to discuss options for his future with us, but the matter ended suddenly a week later when Skinny left and did not return. We figured he had gotten himself in trouble at another house or even with a bigger bear. Or he could have found a lovely female bear to court. Whatever the cause, this time his walkabout was permanent.

Skinny's disappearance led Patti and me to a discussion of whether or not we were corrupting these bears by giving them seeds and human companionship. Were we reducing their natural fear of man? Were we leading them to make bad decisions to trust others as they did us? We thought about this often.

As time passed, however, we had no more of this type of destructive or intrusive behavior from any of our bear friends. Sure, they'd get into the garbage if we left it out, but they never even bothered our garden over the years. And as we began to learn more about bears, we became more discerning about their behavior.

In June, Little Bit also gave up her stay-at-home ways and began to roam. At first, we thought she had gone in search of Skinny, but one day Patti looked out and there she was on the deck. She did not return alone. "Jack, better come out and take a look at this. You're not going to believe it. Our little girl is growing up."

We went out on the back deck and Patti gestured toward the ground below. I peered over the railing, not seeing anything in the tall weeds. Then as I turned I saw him. A big, very big, black male. He cocked his head, almost squinting in the sunlight, looking for Little Bit. Obligingly, she climbed up on the seat, stuck her legs through the railing and started licking the sunflower seeds we had put along the top for the birds. It was her favorite place on the deck. The male bear, idly scratching, turned this way and that, trying to keep track of the numerous chipmunks that darted around him in their frantic haste to get up the stairs and stuff their cheeks full of seeds. Little Bit climbed down, went over to Patti and nosed her hand, looking for her favorite nuts.

"Sorry, baby," Patti crooned, going down on one knee so she could scratch the bear's neck. "I was so excited about your new boyfriend, I forgot to bring your nuts." Little Bit ambled to the stairs, peering down at her new friend. Seeing her, he

A shy suitor waits for Little Bit.

A casual Little Bit relaxes out back.

climbed up two steps, then carefully smelled her neck and muzzle. She licked his nose, the bears forming a picture of newfound love. She pushed past him on her way down the beaten bear trail leading to the creek. Dutifully, he followed until they disappeared from view. Soon we could hear the grating of the rocks as the bear pair slowly made their way across the creek, probably headed for a soft day bed and an afternoon siesta.

"Wow," said Patti, "I feel like a new mother-in-law."

I laughed. "Well, she brought her new boyfriend home in order to show him off. You're right. Our little girl is growing up."

She stayed with her newfound friend about three days, which seems to be typical black-bear mating behavior. After that, she came back and a couple of the young males, primarily Scar, followed her around, but her interest was casual at best.

That month, we purchased a video camera to better capture bear behavior for posterity. I never got to be any good with it, and my first efforts were hilarious.

A yearling cub that had just been dumped by his mother became my first subject. He was a feisty little guy, but not yet very smart in the ways of the world. One overcast Sunday morning, he climbed up a corner post to get some seeds. He'd peek across the deck, I would get close, and he'd retreat back down the post. Then I'd back up and he'd return. Then I'd scare him back down. Finally, I went down the stairs and approached him where he stood holding the post. That confused him. He looked away, pretending I wasn't there. Then he stood up, bowed his neck, and tried a fearsome mock charge, huffing and puffing, all thirty pounds of him. I shot fifteen or twenty minutes of rank amateur footage, then gave up for the day and went up on the deck.

Little Bit was also on her way to the deck, so I sat outside and shot some footage of her. Up the post came the pugnacious cub once more. Little Bit stepped carefully around me, then bluff-charged the cub, sending him sliding down the post. He stayed at the bottom, holding tight, waiting for Little Bit to leave. He was persistent. Somehow, this affront angered the usually mild-mannered female. She peered over the edge and tried to warn him off, first with a glare, then with a couple of huffs and puffs, but as noted, the yearling wasn't so swift. He'd been around a couple of days and still hadn't figured out that the stairway to the deck was a lot easier to climb than the posts. He was the only bear that never figured that out.

Patti came out and saw Little Bit's rump up in the air and her head hanging over the deck. "What's she doing like that? She asked.

"There's a little yearling cub down below," I said. "He's planning to wait her out." We had never seen her really upset at another bear, but she did not like the cub hanging around. He seemed to rub her the wrong way. "Leave him alone, Little Bit," I said. "He's not going to bother you."

At the sound of my voice, she came back over to me and took some seeds from my hand, as if to say she was sorry. She had always recognized her name and would generally come when called, even from a hundred yards away. She also knew Skinny's name and probably other things we were unaware of. So it wasn't unexpected for her to come over to me. What was unexpected was the scrabbling sound of the cub's claws coming back up the post. Oh no, I thought. And sure enough, this time Little Bit had had it. She didn't stop. As soon as she saw the cub's head above the level of the deck, she spun around me and went for him in a rush. Her furor shocked me.

"Little Bit, Little Bit," I called, trying to get her attention.

But she was going after that cub. She struggled to squeeze completely under the bench, then down the post she went. By then, the cub had hurried to a large aspen about twenty-five feet away. He was getting the message. The cub went up the trunk, followed closely by a huffing-puffing Little Bit, a little on the heavy side for tree climbing.

And then, about halfway up the tree with the cub high in the branches above her, Little Bit stopped as much from exhaustion as anything and started to listen to Patti's voice calling her. "Little Bit, come on down and leave that cub alone!" she said, speaking in her stern mother's tone of voice. "Come on, Little Bit, right this minute!" The bear looked down, then up, then back down at Patti clapping her hands. She hesitated, then slowly began to ease herself back down the tree. We often wondered if she was trying to protect us or if it was a territorial issue. Although the cub sat up in the tree until we went inside some fifteen minutes later, Little Bit had by then lost interest and paid him no attention. She instantly became her same old placid self.

That summer, we had started keeping a journal to record the level and nature of bear activity. On the day of Little Bit's tree climb after the cub, my notations show the cub returned five times. Another note tells of the day being windy and the cub uneasy. High winds were a common occurrence, and maybe they were partly to blame for Little Bit's irritability. On blustery days, when the woods were noisy and scents traveled erratically, bears of all ages would get skittish.

In mid-June, I went up to what we laughingly called our garden to do some weeding. Actually, part of the reason I put the garden in was to have a source of funny stories for the paper. Believe me, gardening in those rocky conditions was so awful as to be humorous in and of itself. In several years of trying, I never got one ear of mature corn, not one. The lettuce was rarely edible. The peas and beans were hit and miss. Only root crops like potatoes, carrots, beets, and the like were somewhat successful. And of course, radishes were excellent. I used to say that if there had been a recipe for a radish hot dish, I'd have been a star.

The part of gardening that Little Bit enjoyed most was the hose. She played with it and chewed it, which turned it into a sieve and made watering difficult. What with drought, cold weather, rotten soil, midsummer frosts, and wayward moose tromping around, gardening was an iffy prospect even with a good hose, and after she got done with it, I didn't have one.

Bears are sometimes portrayed as stolid, lumbering loners, but most of them seem to have an intense need to let loose from time to time and simply have fun. As juveniles, they chased and wrestled at every opportunity. Little Bit's hose game was only one of several pastimes she invented over the years for fun. When she and Scar found the shovel I had laid against the shed one day, they played a game of toss with it till they got bored and wandered away.

As for gardening, I did try. As I was down on my hands and knees weeding one cool morning, I looked up to see a yearling cub searching for kernels of corn in the grass. The cub had stopped and looked at me, wondering what kind of animal I was, down there on all fours. A strange one, most likely. At first I thought it was the same cub we'd seen appearing lately around the deck, and I ignored him. Never directly staring at him, I kept my head bent and continued weeding, watching him out of the corner of my eye. But after he moved around a bit, climbed and unclimbed a couple of trees for fear I'd come after him, I saw he was yet another newcomer.

Finally, he cautiously came down the aspen and stood at its base on his hind legs with his front paws firmly holding onto the tree in case an escape route was needed. I started humming, and after about an hour he had ventured within a few feet. He was a curious and handsome little fellow. He hung around and watched what I was doing. By way of conversation, I asked him to help me with the weeding.

Back at the house, I told Patti of my "assistant" up at the garden. We would refer to him as the corn cub and the other one, the one in back, would be called the seed cub. These two yearling cubs were with us on and off throughout the summer, but, strangely, they never spent much time together. One preferred to stay near the corn pile at the garden, while the other was constantly being chased off the deck by bigger bears.

By the middle of the summer of 1992, we had spent almost two years' time observing bears. It was a significant start toward understanding at least some of their behavior. One of the most important lessons was in getting rid of unwanted bears. So far, we had learned three ways. In serious cases, when we truly wanted the bear gone, or when other methods had failed, we'd use the slingshot. Because it gave only a little sting, you might have to hit a bear three or four times before it got the message. Bears have excellent memories, however, so I wouldn't try to befriend one that I'd stung with a slingshot.

For close-in work, like breaking up an argument at the seed box, there was the bear stick, a heavy hardwood stick about three inches in diameter and four feet long. I wouldn't hit the bears with it, just thump it on the decking. It was astonishing how the bears responded just to the weight and heft of that stick and scattered.

But the most effective way to send a bear on its way without harm was a simple show of confidence. This was the ticket out in the open, where you had some room. If you walk steadily at a black bear, no matter what size it is, it will generally break and run, especially if you're a male. Bears can sense the sex of a person. Don't ask me how they know this, but they do. Patti could try the same thing, but it might not work once they figured out she's a female. You don't have to yell, scream, pound on pans, or shout to make this method work. The unfaltering approach is what's important.

Now if you really want to make a scary impression, add something strange to your gait. Glide instead of walk. Or flap your arms like a bird. This will cause even the bravest of bears to bolt.

I cannot guarantee that any of these methods will work on any given bear. They did, however, work for me over a period of six full seasons.

Little Bit immediately understood that when I was armed with the stick or the slingshot, I was there to help her. Usually, it was to clear the deck of arguing males. She would actually get behind me, secure in the knowledge that she would be protected.

However, one day when I was trying to scare off a persistent male, Little Bit wandered out of the woods while I was reloading. I didn't look carefully, just shot at what I thought was the male and hit her instead. When Patti looked down on the lower deck, there was Little Bit licking her hip where she'd been hit. No doubt it stung for a few seconds, but the more serious injury had been done to her feelings. Patti tried calling her in, but it took the bribery of a handful of almonds and a lot of scratching behind her ears to get her to come near. "You should have seen her expression," Patti said to me. "She was pouting and looking at me as if to say, 'How could you let him do that?'"

It was the only mistake of that type I made, and fortunately she soon got over it.

* * *

In mid-July, I noticed a yearling cub in the front yard acting strangely. I couldn't tell if it was one of our regulars, so I called Patti out of the kitchen. "No, I'm sure it's not the seed cub or the corn cub. Why? What's he up to?"

"Just watch for a minute," I said. Within only a few seconds, the bear whirled, ran for the bushes, and fell down. It got up and staggered a bit. Then it shook its head, trying to get its bearings.

"I'm going out and see if I can spot anything wrong with him. Don't worry, I'll be careful." She walked around to look the cub over, but it ran for a tree, not letting her get too close. Finally, when it was clear the cub would stay shy of us, we decided reluctantly that it would either get well or not on its own. There was nothing we could do. He stayed around for a few minutes to drink water and to eat from a pan of seeds Patti put out for him. When he turned to leave, we finally saw he had been shot in the side.

We never saw him alive again, but about a month later, while walking the clearing beneath the rural electric power lines a half mile from home, we found the remains of a cub its size. Only the fur and bones remained. Every bit of meat and tissue had been picked clean. We picked up the skull and the twenty claws and took them home, where they remain today as mementos of the yearling cub.

Blueberry season starts about August 1 and runs for two or three weeks. Being of the wild lowbush variety, the berries can differ widely in quality within a few miles' distance. Patti and I were always on the lookout for promising patches and drove around checking them as they ripened. But for Little Bit, the season always started a week to ten days earlier. Somehow, she would be eating mature blueberries as proven by her blue

Portrait of a young lady bear.

droppings, well in advance of us finding anything ripe. "I don't know where you go, old girl," I said, "but you know where they're at."

Little Bit loved blueberries about as much as any food she could find growing wild. Raspberries, which she also found in abundance, did not interest her unless she was very hungry. Then she might pick a few.

Apples, which were grown by the homesteaders and used primarily in pies and sauces, grow prolifically on the old farms. Some bears get into trouble breaking the branches on apple trees they find in people's yards. Our tree looked like it had gone through a tornado. It wasn't big enough to support a bear, but bears tried to climb it anyway. None of the branches were more than two feet long. Needless to say, the crop was always poor and the bears always beat us to the harvest.

There's no doubt that honey is right at the top of a bear's food list. What people don't realize is that sunflower seeds are up there too. This is the reason so many birdfeeders are destroyed. They're full of seeds and make a prime target. Most bears we knew would sit and eat sunflower seeds for hours if given the chance.

Bear specials on TV always show brown bears catching salmon, but some northern black bears don't even recognize fish as food. When Little Bit and Skinny first came to our house, we gave them a couple of small fish to eat and they played catch with them instead. We also tried fish with several other bears, but they wouldn't touch it either.

Give them a rotten log full of grubs or ants, however, and they are in heaven. Patti and I were driving an overgrown tote road one day and came upon a bear totally engrossed in tearing apart an old log on the road ahead. We kept driving slowly until we were within about twenty feet. The bear looked up in disbelief that we had gotten so close without his noticing, then fled into the bushes.

Sometimes in the spring, a bear would come along and peel back large areas of sod and grass, maybe a yard wide by two yards long, examining the ground beneath it. We saw this behavior many times. At first, we didn't know the exact nature of the food the bears were seeking. Later, we figured it was the treasure troves of sunflower seeds hidden underground by the chipmunks. When a bear would discover a tunnel, it would start to dig, and often the tunnel would be long and complex, with multiple entrances. The bear would use its nose to lead it along the maze to the cache of seeds or nuts at the end.

Sometimes bears would excavate holes two or three feet deep to get at their target.

One day in late summer, Scar was busy digging on the hillside between the lawn and garden. We watched the hole get deeper and wider. Soon, he was down in the hole, digging like a dog. We figured he might be digging a hibernation den, but then he stopped, lay down, and started eating a chipmunk's hidden trove.

Food was scarce that fall and the bears were very hungry. Worried that the males would be attracted to some hunters' baits, Patti and I decided to replenish the corn pile. Immediately, we had all four of our "regular" boys up at the corn pile eating contentedly. To give an idea how much bears consume before hibernation, from September 3 until September 10, a one-week period, we put out 700 pounds of corn. By providing the corn, we also kept the males off the back deck and made it easier for Little Bit to spend the time she wanted to on the deck with us. Much of the time, she seemed content to just hang around.'

That September, we started to notice a change in her personality. She seemed to prefer our company to that of the other bears. One night we came home from a Friday night high school football game to find her lying on her side with her feet pressed firmly against the sliding glass door. At first, we thought something terrible had happened, but she popped her head up as we approached the door and we realized she had just taken a nap while waiting for us. Her feet were against the door so she'd feel it slide open and wake up when we came outdoors.

Although only mid-September, there was frost on the handrail and I could see my breath in the crisp night air. We decided to sit outside with her for a few minutes in the moonlight. She seemed to want the company. Perhaps she knew

Little Bit and Patti on the back deck.

she'd be going in a couple of days and was trying to say good-bye for the season.

Within five minutes, we heard the wolves start howling off to the west, not far away. Their haunting calls, a dissonant chorus that the pack kept up for several minutes, never failed to raise the hairs on my neck. The sound is so utterly wild and heard in so few places, yet there we sat in the darkness with a

Patti and Little Bit.

bear who listened to its nuances even more intently than we did. Soon after the wolves started their melancholy serenade, Little Bit got up ponderously and moved slowly across the deck to leave. Perhaps the wolves had reminded her of things she had to do before she could hibernate safely that fall.

As September passed, all our "regulars" left to hibernate. Little Bit's last day was the fifteenth, and Scar was the last to leave on the twenty-fifth. Normally, we wouldn't see any more bears till the following season, but late September and early October brought wanderers from afar.

One night, three adults and a yearling cub came and went. The seed cub came back a couple of times, joined by a small female we called the Little Girl bear. She had a face that was easy to recognize, sort of pushed in, and eyes that seemed to cross. For about ten days, she stayed very close. She even took to sleeping on the deck. After fattening up, she left on October 7.

We don't know why that bear was in the terrible condition she was. She may have been sick, or her foraging had gone poorly. But the last night Little Girl bear was around that fall, she was an unwitting participant in an episode involving the largest black bear we had ever seen or have ever seen since. She was on the deck after dark when she was joined by a pair of juvenile males who looked to be identical. The threesome seemed to be getting along just fine when suddenly, Little Girl began to shy away. Soon she had retreated up onto the handrail at the edge of the deck and could go no further. The handrail was about four feet off the deck and fourteen feet off the ground, so a fall would have been dangerous, even fatal.

At that moment, an enormous black bear walked into the light on the deck. Patti and I were literally speechless. The bear was not fat, just huge. His fur was prime. He looked at Little Girl, then dropped his head and took a mouthful of seeds. The young males fled. She tried to creep along the six-inch-wide handrail to make her escape, but the big bear looked up and something in his glance made her retreat again.

Meanwhile, he was standing broadside, and I was able to judge his height and length in relation to marks on the backrest and railing behind him. When I later went out to take measurements, using the signposts I'd lined up visually, I found his height along the back to be thirty-nine inches, or ten inches taller than a typical desk, and his body length, not including head or tail, to be fifty-eight inches, or nearly five feet. I'm sure that a bear researcher could extrapolate a weight from that, but our guess was about 600 pounds. While this may sound like a lot, it is far less than the weight of the record black bear of all time, a Minnesota specimen who weighed 813 pounds.

Finally, Patti despaired of Little Girl's situation and decided to take matters into her own hands. She cracked open the door and shoved a broom out at the huge visitor. While this didn't scare off the bear, it did redirect his attention, which allowed Little Girl literally to tiptoe along the rail and make her escape. Fortunately, he seemed a mild enough fellow and did not attempt to eat the broom or smash the sliding glass door. When Little Girl had slipped by, Patti withdrew the broom and we closed the door, shut the blinds, turned out the light, and said goodbye to the bears for another season.

By that fall, we knew enough about bears to know that Little Bit would not be returning alone the next summer. We called a nationally known bear expert to find out how many cubs we might expect to see in the spring, and he said a lot would depend on a female's weight when she hibernates. He gave us weight ranges but explained that since I had no way to weigh her, the weight variables wouldn't help us much. I wrote them down anyway.

I also asked a question that had been troubling us all summer. How would Little Bit behave toward us if she had a cub or cubs to protect? Would she still be the same bear? "Yes indeed," our consultant responded. "How she acts around you without cubs is how she'll act with cubs. She'll still be the same. If she trusted you before, she'll trust you after." With that advice, we started the long vigil until spring.

4

LIFE IN THE
SANCTUARY

When we arrived in Minnesota, all the squirrels gave us wide berth, but over the years, Patti made friends with an especially personable red squirrel who would come running to her when called. She named the squirrel Bertha (we often referred to her as "Bertha Squirrel"), and there was no question that this particular animal was queen of the back deck.

First, she was aggressive. She would clear the deck of all squirrels and chipmunks before she would settle down to enjoy herself. Sometimes, her charge was so sudden that her victims would launch themselves into midair rather than face her in combat. Surprisingly, they always survived the ten-foot fall.

Second, she was tenacious. She would chase another squirrel for an hour if necessary to drive it away. Patti sometimes watched as the chase went from tree to tree, limb to limb, in such a fashion that would make a trapeze artist envious.

Yet around us, Bertha Squirrel was gentle and playful. In winter, she would race across the snow, bound up the steps, and jump onto the snow shovel for a ride as Patti shoveled the deck.

In the summer, when the red-tailed hawks would soar overhead, Bertha would climb to the top of the roof and chatter furiously at them, thinking she was invincible and could drive them off. Patti would stand helplessly below, calling her to come down.

One day, we brought home a couple of especially promising pieces of driftwood from a remote trout lake. Patti sat out on the back deck with a jackknife, carving the rotted portions away and etching the natural lines of the wood. It took about three hours, most of the afternoon. As Patti worked I could hear her talking to Bertha Squirrel. It wasn't a one-sided conversation, however, as Bertha could also be heard chattering politely back. She had joined Patti early that afternoon and stayed by her side, and on her knee, all the time she was carving. Finally, the little squirrel wrapped herself in her tail and simply watched, interrupting her stay only a couple of times to chase off unwanted squirrel and chipmunk intruders.

We'd been close to Bertha for three years and could pretty much expect her to come and sit with us when called. She preferred Patti's lap, and as Patti would say, "That little squirrel gladdens my heart."

One Saturday in early May of 1993, I was sitting out on the front walkway enjoying the morning sun when Bertha Squirrel came running toward me. "What are you doing out in front, Bertha?" I asked.

But, Bertha was busy. She ran right past me into the garage, where she jumped up on the cluttered workbench. Then she returned to where I was sitting, climbed up the corner of the house, and disappeared into a small hole. By now, she had my attention, so I turned and watched the hole. Soon, a smaller squirrel clambered out, clinging to the wall. It was one of Bertha's babies and when she appeared right behind it, I could see it was about one-fourth her size, a perfect squirrel in miniature.

She grabbed the baby in her mouth and carefully eased down the wall, then made her way across the yard and into the garage. When she had disappeared, I went inside and called Patti to come quickly. I told her it was Bertha Squirrel and her babies. Naturally, Patti was out in a flash.

We peeked into the garage to see Bertha deposit her first baby in one of the two snowmobile helmets lying on the workbench. Then we sat on the walkway while she repeated the trip with a second baby, then a third, a fourth, and a fifth. It was awesome to see this little red squirrel carry her young down walls, up walls, across gravel, and through the grass.

Finally, after the five young squirrels had been carefully deposited in the two helmets, creating an instant squirrel playpen, Bertha came over and flopped down on her belly next to Patti. "What a wonderful bunch of babies you've raised, Bertha," Patti said, gently scratching and petting the tired mother. "But no one ever said motherhood is easy."

Thereafter, Bertha Squirrel and her babies primarily lived on the top floor of the garage, and Patti regularly put seeds in the loft for them. To the best of our knowledge, they never damaged anything. They did, however, leave the hulls of some sunflower seeds in a couple of my old boots, and when one day I went to put one on, I got a surprise.

After a winter of watchful expectation, intensified in the spring by the incessant questions of subscribers and neighbors, the bears finally began to come back. Surprisingly, Little Bit, now starting her fifth summer, our fourth, was among the first to arrive. She made her appearance just as the forest was leafing out in its many shadings of light and delicate greens. With her was a gangly male cub. We were thrilled.

She marched right over to the sliding door and placed her muddy paws against the glass to announce her presence. Patti opened it excitedly. The cub took one look at her and fled off the deck and up the old spruce tree. Little Bit was happy to see us but didn't seem to have much interest in her cub. As for the cub, he wanted nothing to do with us. We'd go out and he'd run off into the woods.

Thus began the strange summer of 1993. When Little Bit came onto the deck, she seemed to ignore the cub entirely. When she left the deck, the cub in turn would pay her little attention, seeming perfectly happy to go his own way. The cub would lead his mother through the woods, then climb a tree and snooze the day away, leaving her wondering what to do with him.

One day we watched as Little Bit, by now a 250-pound bear, sat at the base of the old spruce tree by the deck, waiting for her cub to come down. She had been sitting patiently all morning and was losing the battle of wills with the stubborn cub, who was only about a tenth of her size but who was clearly in charge. It was not the first time. Finally impatient, Little Bit stood up, grasped the base of the tree, and began to climb. She shinnied up the trunk, then struggled though the maze of branches.

As she approached the cub, he looked down, understood her intent, and climbed higher. She kept after him, neared the top of the tree, and put a paw up to pull him down to her. He edged higher, finally reaching the topmost limb, which was no more than a supple stick. Seeing that the limb would not support her, she hesitated, then stopped. After a few moments' deliberation, she retreated down the tree. At the bottom, she threw herself against the trunk in obvious frustration.

Later, Patti looked back out the sliding door and shook her

head. "She's still lying there. She looks hot and she's panting. I'm going to go out and sit with her for a while." She grabbed a can of Cutter's from the fireplace mantle, then went out across the back deck to the base of the tree where Little Bit sat. "Little Bit, you poor baby, you're uncomfortable sitting on these rocks right in the sun. Why won't that silly cub mind you? Maybe you should just go off and leave him here."

She looked up to where the cub, whom we had now named Miracle (as in, it will be a miracle if he survives), was stretched across several branches in the shade. He appeared to be sleeping. I looked out at my wife sitting with the female bear. They were as compatible with each other as two creatures could be. There was total trust and understanding between them.

Bertha Squirrel and Miracle.

Clearly, Little Bit's sensitive nature had allowed her cub to get the upper hand. When she clunked deep in her throat (as mother bears do to call their cubs), he ignored her. Instead of her leading little Miracle through the woods, it was she who followed him. When male bears threatened, she retreated. Sometimes, she even climbed a tree right behind her cub. Compared to other mother bears we had met and observed, she was meek and uncertain. In spite of these qualities, or perhaps because of them, she was always our special bear.

For several weeks, mother–cub relations continued in the same vein. Little Bit was happy, but Miracle was not. Then for a period of two weeks, they vanished. Near the end of that time, I talked to Ed Hedstrom, our neighbor about a half mile south, who told me that about a week earlier his two golden retrievers had treed a bear he thought was Little Bit, plus a cub. Patti and I were worried and confused. What was Little Bit up to? Why didn't she come back to the deck?

She finally returned, but then kept losing her cub. Patti went along with her several times to look for Miracle in the forest. It seemed Little Bit couldn't remember what tree she'd put him up. She'd head for an aspen and look up, then proceed to a clump of birch for a sniff. But, no, it must be that red pine. And on and on. She was as confused as he was uncooperative. What a mess. As we watched, day after day, the cause of her confusion became evident. She would put her cub up a tree, then leave to come visit us. He would climb down, wander away, then climb another tree. No wonder she couldn't find him. Every tree was a potential hiding place. It was truly a miracle she ever found the little rascal at all.

Naturally, Little Bit's difficulties caused us to wonder if her poor parenting skills were a result of our relationship with her. At that time, we had no answers.

* * *

Little Bit and Bertha Squirrel share a line of sunflower seeds.

This was also the spring our old Labrador, Ramah, died. We buried her on the sunlit hillside near the garden shed where the snow had melted, then marked the grave with a small cairn of rocks we found nearby.

I went up a couple of days later to check the grave. At the site, my eye caught a strange shape, which I made out to be a coyote, curled up as if asleep against a wall of the shed. It was only ten feet away, so I stood looking for any sign of breathing or motion. There was none. The coyote was old and gaunt. Somehow, it had picked this specific place to lie down and die.

Patti and I always wondered if the coyote could smell or in some way sense the dog nearby. It was a strange coincidence. We think the coyote was probably the same one who had been around the house, on and off, for several years. He had often marked the snow near the house in an effort to interest Ramah. A case of unrequited love.

No more than a week later, we drove to Barron, Wisconsin, and bought a pair of twelve-week-old female German shepherds from a breeder. We named them Sheba and Shadow and collectively referred to them as the "Shepherd Sisters."

To give them a place to be outside, yet separate from the bears, we built a seven-foot cedar fence around a part of the side yard. With the fence in place, we had no fears the dogs would chase deer or get in trouble with the bears. A fellow who worked at the newspaper office helped to build the fence. At one point in the construction project, I left him standing on a stepladder while I went to get us more nails. Little Bit picked that exact moment to come up toward the deck. The sight of someone standing on a stepladder right in her usual path unnerved her completely. She ran huffing and puffing to the back door, where she stood up and scratched the door desperately. When Patti went out to see what was causing the problem, Little Bit huddled behind her. It took a lot of affection to reassure the bear that all was well.

Meanwhile, having caught sight of the bear, our helper left his post in a hurry. I found him at his truck. When I asked him why he'd left, he muttered something about getting a cigarette, seeing as how there was a bear around the backyard anyway.

Little Girl bear, pitifully thin when she had arrived late the previous September, came back this year herding three splendid little cubs weighing about five pounds apiece. We knew it was her from her size and those unmistakable eyes. The cubs were about the size of toy poodles, and we agreed they were the cutest little balls of fluff we had ever seen.

Almost immediately, Little Girl had a confrontation with a strange male bear who was passing through. Although smaller than the male, she chased him high into a tall birch and kept him there a half hour. We were astonished that the small, timid female bear we'd known could suddenly turn so ferocious. Then we thought some more. Could this be the mother bear we'd called "Crazy Bear?"

Her size was right, her general shape was the same, and the number of cubs was accurate. We'd heard that new mothers usually don't have triplets, which meant these cubs were most likely not her first.

All the signs pointed to the probability that Little Girl and Crazy Bear were one and the same. After watching her in action, we certainly believed it. So in honor of her new identity, we gave her a new name. From now on, she'd be known as Big Mama, certainly not for her size, but for the size of her heart.

In contrast to Little Bit's difficulties, Big Mama had the control of a drill sergeant over her brood. Just at dark every evening, she would bring them up on deck for about five minutes, then take them to a nearby tree and send them scampering up by standing at the base of the trunk on her hind legs and slapping it with her front paws. Then she'd return alone for a leisurely snack of her own.

At this point, we were reminded of our discussion the previous fall about how many cubs could be expected. Little Bit, now a large female, had returned with only one cub, while Big Mama, who weighed no more than half as much as Little Bit, had had three. Over the years, the relationship between the size of our three females with their combined total of five litters didn't subscribe to any rhyme or reason we could detect. Apparently, a mother bear's total body weight when she dens is not the best predictor of her cub-bearing capability.

With her cubs, Big Mama was generally a nocturnal visitor. She rarely came by in daylight. She would walk up on the deck and get our attention, then when we opened the sliding glass door, she would sit in such a way as to block the steps to

Big Mama and her trio.

the deck. No other bears could walk up onto the deck unless they went through Big Mama.

The "babies," as I called them, were charmers. If you didn't look too closely, you'd swear they were furry little puppies. They would literally dive into my arms and lick me with their soft tongues as I reached out for them. It was impossible not to love them, as opposed to Miracle, who would still not stay on the deck when we were present.

More than once we had seen Big Mama in action, protecting her cubs ferociously, yet she showed complete trust with us around them. She also deferred to Little Bit when possible, and to our knowledge they never fought. We often wondered if perhaps Big Mama was Little Bit's mother and if Little Bit had grown up on our land about the time we moved there. But of course there were no answers.

That year, on the Fourth of July, we had a normal assortment of visitors, including a new two-year-old we called Clancy, along with our regulars Scar and Sarge, and a rare daylight visit by Big Mama and her gang.

At 8:45 P.M. our power suddenly went out. It was still daylight, but we got out the candles, kerosene lamps, and flashlights to prepare for the worst. At that time, we didn't know if the outage was general or localized. Despite living in an isolated situation with miles of electrical grid strung through the wilderness, we were rarely without power.

I called Arrowhead Electric Cooperative and got through to their emergency number. They said there had been no other calls, so the problem must just lie with us. They said someone would be coming by to take a look. It was a beautiful, quiet evening, so we sat on the deck until ten o'clock, when it was almost nightfall and we could hear the rockets and feel the concussion bombs of the fireworks display six miles away in Grand Marais.

It was completely dark. We had lighted the kerosene lanterns when the power crew arrived at 11:30. They checked a couple of things, then said it was a blown fuse or breaker on the junction pole a quarter-mile north. "Probably a squirrel or bird," said one of the repairmen.

I thought for a second, then asked, "Could it be a bear cub?"

"Yes, we've had one of those already this summer," he answered. "We'll let you know." They set off up the trail toward the main power line. At midnight, they returned with the bad news. "It was a cub all right. Found it dead at the base of the pole." They said they were afraid the mother bear might still be around, so they were eager to get out of there.

They switched the lights back on and left. I broke the sad news to Patti. This was like losing a member of the family. To our knowledge, there were no other cubs around our immediate area, except for Miracle and Big Mama's trio.

We went to bed wondering who the victim was, and in the morning, the identity of the dead cub was revealed. Little Bit arrived with Miracle, and later Big Mama with two cubs. So it was one of hers. Perhaps it was my imagination, but she seemed for the first time to need the security of our back deck.

Like other mothers, she had taught the cubs to run from one tree to the next, to be always ready to climb at the slightest hint of danger. Where situated, those poles were the only things to climb, but with deadly consequences.

We had never named Big Mama's cubs, so we immediately named the two who remained. The surviving boy became Napoleon, and the female, Honey. Napoleon earned his sobriquet because you could hear him coming a quarter-mile away. He would bray and squall at the slightest excuse, trying to be the boss. Still, he always obeyed his mother.

The next morning, we fashioned homemade sets of windchimes and hung them from several electric poles to frighten the cubs away. We don't know how well they worked, but no other cub was killed that summer.

Scar came once or twice in mid-May, then left for a month before returning. Was he out looking for a girl bear? Was he exploring the country? Sometimes, it's impossible to figure why bears do what they do.

Napoleon and Honey, Big Mama's two surviving cubs.

Scar showed up at the end of June and immediately got into a fight with an aggressive stranger coming down the driveway. The two adult males bowed their necks to make themselves look bigger. Then both raised themselves on their hind legs, wrestling, cuffing, and trying to bite each other. After about five minutes, combat ceased, and the bears went their separate ways, off into the woods.

Never having seen a real bear fight before, we didn't know whether or not their encounter was warfare or just extremely aggressive play. There appeared to be no injuries, but Scar came back soon after, while the other bear never reappeared. We thought of Scar as Sir Galahad from that day forward for his spirited defense of the home territory.

Among the males, Scar was the gentlest and friendliest. He would hold his own against the other males when a fight was

Scar looked large and fierce, but was very gentle.

threatened, but he seemed to understand the two mother bears and their need for space better than the other boys. By now, Scar was full grown and quite a hunk. Patti got along well with him, sitting with him on the deck. He would go right to her.

However, something about him bothered me. He always

approached me cautiously, knowing that I was also a male. In fact, he crept toward me in a stealthy way that made me uneasy. Patti thought he was simply on his guard, but I was never sure. Maybe I'd shot him with the slingshot and he remembered. At any rate, I usually kept him at arm's length.

Scar gave the lie to the concept that bears are loners. He was always looking to hang out with the other bears as Skinny had done two summers earlier. We'd be sitting out with Little Bit and along would come Scar. You could almost see his anticipation at the chance to get together.

"Come on, Scar," I'd say, "give us a break. This is Little Bit's time." He would turn around and amble into the woods, only to return in five or ten minutes, as if to say, "Is it time now?"

I remember reading a book once which postulated that if you put a bear and a hunter in a one-square-mile wooded area, the bear would see the hunter every day, but the hunter would probably never see the bear. Bears do not crash around in their normal day-to-day activities. In fact, they can move like ghosts. When they choose, they can travel through the forest in near silence, especially in areas where they have established paths or "tunnels" through the brush. Our bears made tunnels through the brush between the deck and the creek. Once a bear started through the maze of tunnels, we could look and listen intently but see and hear nothing. The bear would simply vanish until he came out the other end a hundred feet away.

I've always had excellent hearing, probably to compensate for Mr. Magoo eyesight. But Patti and I would sit on the back deck in late summer when the creek was quiet and bears such as Scar or Little Bit would come out of the forest, walk across the lower deck area, climb the steps, and walk out onto the deck not six feet away, and we would hear nothing. Zero. Surprised us every time.

* * *

Bears are big, powerful creatures who sometimes never realize the extent of their force. As a result, they can often be frightened and even defeated by the most unlikely things.

That summer, we had drawn a sizable herd of chipmunks to the back deck, where they loved to come up and eat sunflower seeds. Chipmunks don't get along with each other very well, and after a year or so of cohabitation they display awful scars and other imperfections. Our favorite, Chester, had half a tail. A couple of others were missing a tail and an ear, respectively. They just liked to fight.

One day, a strange bear showed up to sneak some seeds just as chipmunks in the seed box were being attacked by other chipmunks coveting seeds. The chippers paid no attention to the bear. The bear was a little nervous anyway, and as he crept across the deck, a major chipmunk battle erupted. Suddenly chippers were racing everywhere—between his legs, behind him and in front of him. Frantic, he bolted. One minute he had been padding nonchalantly toward a delicious meal and the next he was fleeing, tail tucked, an unwitting loser in the Chipmunk War.

Another strange bear, the first and only cinnamon-colored bear to visit us, fell victim to ducks at the corn pile. Several times a year, in the spring and fall and after their babies were raised, the mallards would fly in for a mid-day snack. One morning while the cinnamon bear was lying down eating at the corn pile, a flock of about two dozen mallards flew in. If you've ever seen a mallard crash-land on dry ground, you know what a loud and disorganized event it can be. The bear was briefly startled and retreated a few feet before reclaiming his rightful place at the corn. Having regained his composure, Mr. Bear remained standing as he munched determinedly and kept a wary eye on the ducks some twenty feet away.

Hungry ducks can make a lot of noise. So with loud quacks, they began their advance and formed a semicircle around the feeding bear. Again, he backed off. This time, though, as he backed up, the ducks came forward, which further unnerved Mr. Bear.

If he had been a deer, he would simply have walked toward the ducks and scattered them. Unaware of this tactic, he stood looking at the apparently fearless ducks for a couple of minutes, then wandered away.

One by one, four nearly full-grown male bears appeared on the back deck, where by July, they were hanging around in a group. They'd lie down in a circle, surrounding the large wooden box of sunflower seeds, then croon a high-pitched single note and blow at each other in an attempt to get the most seeds. Bears can actually lengthen their noses a bit, making them more prominent in this sort of confrontation. As a result of this behavior, we called the gluttonous quartet "the long noses."

Big Mama easily drove the foursome off with her motherly fury, but Little Bit had more trouble. Sometimes, she would chase one off, only to find another up on the deck when she returned. Then her cub would be up a tree and she'd be unable to get back to it or get back on the deck.

That's when I took the trusty bear stick, loaded my slingshot, and went out to help. Although Little Bit was getting bigger each summer, she'd often get behind me on the deck for protection. She somehow thought I was invincible, so I tried to act the part. I'd rant and rave at the "long noses," pound the stick, and ultimately shoot the slingshot. Then I'd stand outside on guard duty while being consumed by mosquitoes. I'd look back after a few minutes, and there would sit Little Bit, casually eating seeds and expecting continued protection.

Meanwhile, her Miracle would be happily snoozing atop a tree, apparently the only place he felt completely safe.

Once or twice each summer, we'd see a fisherman working his way up or down Elbow Creek, tossing a fly or worm into the deeper holes where the small brook trout stayed cool in the shadows of the large granite boulders.

One day, just after Little Bit and Miracle had left, Patti spotted a fly fisherman wading upstream. She went out on the porch and waved. He was busy with his fishing, so she yelled at him, "Hi there!"

He looked up and saw this woman waving at him, so he waved back pleasantly. "Please watch out for the bears," she hollered. "Don't hurt them, especially the mother and her cub."

He didn't hear what she was saying, so he cupped his ear. She explained more loudly, "There's a mother bear and her cub just upstream." For emphasis, she pointed ahead of where he was fishing. This time, he heard the message, interpreted it the way most people would, and went splashing back down the stream as fast as he could go.

With high summer came warm weather and the colorful blanket of yellow buttercups, white daisies, and orange hawk-weed that would cover the rolling meadows. There was plenty of food most years for the bears. By early August, they'd be ravenous, and they'd travel for a week or more at a time to the blueberry patches.

Since the bears' schedules were erratic and unpredictable, we'd never know which, if any, we'd see. When we invited guests for dinner, we'd hope they'd get a glimpse of a bear, but we never knew in advance. Usually, though, Little Bit or one of her friends would arrive on the scene to disrupt the dinner. This happened again and again.

* * *

Dave Lincoln, an old friend, brought his fiancée, Jean, to the North Shore on a sightseeing trip. When they came over for dinner, Toby immediately came by for a "photo op." Then, as soon as we sat down to eat, Little Bit arrived as if by schedule. Dinner was halted while everyone watched her for half an hour. We returned to cold food. At evening's end, Dave pronounced the meal good, and added, "but the floor show was terrific."

That summer we also had a Saturday garage sale. Many of the people who came that morning were more interested in news of Little Bit than in our sale. "Where is she?" They'd ask. "Can we see her?" She was very shy around strangers most of the time, especially when cars were coming and going, doors slamming. It would have taken supernatural power to bring her out in the middle of all that chaos.

In August, when the air was warm and humid enough to feel the weight of every breath, something finally clicked in Miracle's brain and the stubborn cub started to show a marked change in behavior. We could make no sense of the cause or timing. One day, as usual, he was up a distant tree, where he would stay rooted, and then the next day, out of the blue, he was constantly at his mother's side, eating seeds and allowing us to sit outside while he did so. The transformation took place after they had returned from a couple of extended visits to the blueberry patches. With me, Miracle remained a bit shy, hiding behind Little Bit when I came close. Patti was able to sit next to him when his mother was present. But as soon as Little Bit would leave the deck to chase away a smaller bear, he would hightail it to the tall trees far back in the forest.

Miracle had an uncanny ability to frustrate his mother. No sooner had he become somewhat sociable than he discovered new ways to disrupt her life. Little Bit liked to eat seeds from a small, two sided-box we set on the bench. When filled, it would contain two or three pounds of seeds. She would sit on the floor, legs splayed, and hold the box with one arm while she munched and looked around.

One side of the little box had a hole through which passed an old piece of frayed rope—a perfect handle for a mischievous cub. One day Miracle decided to pull the box away from his mother, tugging it about two feet along the bench, as if to say, "Ha ha, I've got it now." She leaned over and pulled it back gently, as if to reply, "No problem. Everything's cool. I'll just take the box back now."

Miracle was stubborn. He grabbed the rope in his teeth and pulled the box even farther away from his mother. The gleam in his eye was unmistakable. It belonged to a small bear-sized Dennis the Menace. She looked at him for a moment, then got up ponderously and walked over to the seed box, where she sat down and took control once more. We had been watching and Patti said, "That is the most patient mother bear in the world. Miracle is without a doubt the most frustrating cub I've ever seen." Things were quiet briefly, then Miracle again went for the rope. "He's a determined little devil," I said.

But this time, as he grabbed the rope, Little Bit was ready. She held the box with her left paw, and with her right she delivered a swat that sent her cub head over heels. He retreated with a whimper. "Wow," Patti said enthusiastically. "She finally let him have it."

Little Bit went back to munching contentedly and Miracle stayed well away from her until about a half-hour later, when she got up and walked to the steps. This time Miracle followed dutifully. After more than a year, Little Bit was finally starting to get the hang of this mother business.

That very night, Little Bit showed just how maternal she

could be. We'd heard the sound of heavy bear feet thundering across the deck, followed by braying and crooning, so we quickly got flashlights and flipped on the back light. There was a large male bear on the deck, a stranger, whom we chased off.

When Patti shined her light around down below to see if anyone was around or to find out what was going on, she discovered Little Bit sitting with her back against the old white spruce tree, holding her frightened cub in her lap with both paws wrapped around him. It was the kind of posture you'd expect to see from a human mother, tender yet defensive. Most people don't realize that a bear can be so sensitive.

Little Bit's favorite snacks consisted of shelled, unsalted nuts we bought at the store. It was a fortunate coincidence that each year, we also got almonds from Patti's dad, Alex. At first, he had sent them as a treat for Patti and me, but as soon as he learned that Little Bit also loved them, he shifted gears. In Palo Alto, California, where he lived, he found a farmer's market right near a grove that sold bulk nuts at a reasonable price. Thenceforth, he would ship a couple of large boxes full of them for "Little Bit" Becklund, which greatly amused the folks at the post office. Little Bit loved those California almonds more than just about anything, especially when she could eat them from our hands.

To see where the bears traveled, and to bring to light other bear-related facts, we made three or four loops around our property each summer. We'd walk the trails, cutting through the thick alder swamps and hazelbrush and checking for signs of passage. In this way, we'd learn the bears' favorite avenues of approach, the location of their beds, and various areas they'd been frequenting.

It always seemed that Little Bit would appear from nowhere as soon as we slid the door open and stepped out on the deck. We wondered how she could anticipate our actions. As we discovered, it had nothing to do with guesswork or luck. We found several fresh daybeds in the deep grass near the power line not more than fifty yards from the back door. She was lying close enough to actually hear us pouring the seeds, then would come a-running.

Eventually we found answers to many behavioral patterns we thought of as mysteries. One of our constant fears was that mother bear and babies would somehow get separated and not find each other. For instance, if Napoleon were to continue eating seeds five minutes after his mother and sister left, he might never catch up to them again. We needn't have worried. Their sense of smell was keen. Only Little Bit managed to lose her cub, and that's because he would take off like a three-year-old at the grocery store, as soon as her back was turned. He might go a block or a mile, and with her poor vision, she could only track him down with her sense of smell.

One Saturday morning in mid-September, Patti heard a familiar sound of bear claws on bark and looked outside. "Oh, oh," she said. "We've got a standoff."

"Okay, I'll get the bear stick and come out," I said. This wasn't the first time, and wouldn't be the last, that Little Bit and Miracle ran into Big Mama, Napoleon, and Honey on the back deck. Sometimes these standoffs were easily resolved, sometimes not. On the day in question, we had three cubs up three separate trees peeking out through the yellowing leaves of aspen and birch. Little Bit was on the deck and Big Mama down below.

We simply needed to move Big Mama back about twenty-five feet so Little Bit could escape. That much accomplished, events would unfold by themselves. Big Mama would come up

Big Mama's Napoleon.

Napoleon sticks out his tongue for more honey.

for seeds, then leave, clunking as she went to get her two kids down from their trees to follow her. Then Little Bit could return to the deck and Miracle could do whatever he pleased. "Okay, Big Mama," I said, thumping the base of the pole on the deck a couple of times for emphasis. "Time to back up. Get back now and give Little Bit some room." I'd point into the woods and, sure enough, Big Mama seemed to understand. Meanwhile Patti was rounding up Little Bit with a handful of nuts, a bribe that always seemed to work.

The plan of action was quite successful in the daylight. It was much more complicated after dark, when it was hard to be sure which bear was where. We always had about a dozen flashlights set around the house, and Patti was careful to make sure they always had fresh batteries for occasions like this.

5

THE GUNS OF
SEPTEMBER

About the twentieth of August, 1993, Napoleon and Honey left unexpectedly with Big Mama. We assumed they were making one last trip to the berry patches. Time passed, until bear hunting season opened on September 1, always a day we dreaded. Where were the bears? We heard gunshots in the evening, which worried us even more.

September 2 came and went. Little Bit and Miracle were hanging around safe and sound, but there was still no sign of Big Mama and her cubs. On September 3, more gunshots could be heard at suppertime. We figured surely the bears had run into trouble. But at 9:30 P.M. the missing trio came trooping across the creek and out of the woods.

Hearing the rocks grating as the bears climbed out of the creek bed, Patti and I hurried outside, wondering who was approaching. When Big Mama and her cubs came up out of the darkness, we cheered in celebration. "Come on you little rascals," I called, feeling genuinely moved by their return.

Patti snuggled the cubs as they climbed into her arms,

then went inside to make up a bucket of condensed milk as a special treat. They appeared to be as happy to see us as we were to welcome them back.

Bear hunting season was always a terrible ordeal during our summers with the bears. Hunters were allowed to put out bait two weeks in advance of opening day. Bait consisted of meat, fish, honey, dog food, syrup, jam, and anything else hunters thought a bear might like.

Most hunters sat in tree stands overlooking their bait, then shot the bear as it came along to eat. Naturally, bears are ravenous by late summer. And during the years when natural foods are in short supply, they are easily attracted to bait.

Approximately 3,400 bears are killed in Northern Minnesota each September in this manner. Although a hunter for many years, I would never hunt any animal in this way because neither skill nor sportsmanship is involved. As far as I'm concerned, bearbaiting should be outlawed. Fortunately, bears are highly intelligent. After the first weekend, they catch on and very few are killed later in the month.

Although we feared for the safety of the bears during hunting season, few were actually lost to legitimate hunters. Over the years, Patti and I estimated that many more were killed by rural homeowners who shot bears simply because they didn't want them around.

It was heartbreaking to see bears wounded by shooters. Several such animals passed our way during those years.

In mid-September, a large male hauled himself across the creek one evening and collapsed on the back lawn. He was obviously badly wounded in the shoulder, so we took a large bowl of sunflower seeds to him. He limped into the woods when we came toward him, but returned a few minutes later to eat. As dusk fell, we heard him struggling through the woods to find a protected place. We never saw him again, although I walked through the forest the next morning to look for him.

Some bears that are wounded like this but still able to escape end up dead in a few days. They are also lost to the hunters, who generally have neither the skill nor the courage to track them through the woods, still green and thick with leaves that time of year. What a terrible waste.

That fall, the berry crop was not just excellent, it was virtually inexhaustible if you were a dedicated picker. With such food plentiful, the bear hunting was poor. On the morning of September 4, long after the usual end of berry picking, we picked three quarts of huge blueberries in thirty minutes. Driving down the old logging road to get to the patch, Patti and I noticed several piles of bear scat. It was all dark blue, with hard little unripe blueberries inside. No wonder there were few bears to be seen around the house, except for the two mothers and their cubs. And no wonder Big Mama and company had been gone so long. They were all still out in the berry patches, having a fine old time.

Meanwhile, we had been busy putting out the newspaper, which included a weekly report by the Sheriff's Department on calls they had answered. Around the end of August, these calls tended to include a number of "bear complaints" from people who lived in Grand Marais.

Almost every year from late August until the first of October, residents could expect to see or hear bears foraging through their neighborhoods at night for food. Sometimes, these visitors even found their way downtown, where they usually rummaged through restaurant Dumpsters. During our years at the newspaper, we received numerous calls about cubs treed by dogs or about adult bears "scaring" children. Actually, the parents were usually more frightened than their kids were, and responded accordingly.

The more fortunate bears managed to get back into the woods alive. Some did not. Mostly, however, the residents stayed calm when the bears hit the vicinity. They were accustomed to an occasional moose cantering down the streets, coyotes on the harbor ice in winter, an eagle mixing in with the seagulls at the fishing docks, and even a few cougar sightings at the edge of town. Bears were simply a fact of life in Grand Marais every year around Labor Day.

6

LITTLE BIT RETURNS
EARLY

On the tenth of May 1994, Patti and I were watching TV in the early evening on our new satellite dish when we heard the wooden steps groan out back. "A bear, do you suppose?" I thought out loud.

Patti got up to go into the living room for a look. "Whoa!" she exclaimed. "Are you who I think you are? Jack, come see. I think we've got Little Bit back already."

I hurried for a look. Sure enough, there was our star boarder sitting by the door, gently scratching the glass with one paw to get our attention. Miracle was behind her, walking along the bench. Patti brought seeds to put outside for Little Bit, but when she reached the door, the bear spun on her rump and walked over to the bench, where she looked out through the trees at the creek.

"Come on, Little Bit," Patti called. "I've got seeds here for you." The bear walked slowly over and got a scratch on the scruff of her neck from my wife, but instead of eating, continued on to the steps and went down. Miracle followed closely behind.

"Well, what was that all about?" I wondered. "She acted like she hardly knew us." I confess that her abrupt departure had disappointed me.

"She knew us all right," Patti replied. "She just seemed preoccupied, like she wanted to drop by and say hello, then get on with something else."

"They sure weren't hungry," I added. I hoped Little Bit had simply smelled or heard something that bothered her, and that she'd be back shortly. My hope vanished when she didn't come back that night or the next.

The days piled up and we saw nothing of Little Bit or Miracle or any other bear. Finally, ten days later, they returned. Once again, it was a "hi and bye" stop. Little Bit looked good, healthy and large, but she did not want to stay around. We couldn't understand any of this behavior.

Then three days later, on May 23, Little Bit returned alone. No cub, but this time she was content to hang around and sit on the bench in the sunshine. She got up and wandered off twice, but each time she returned quickly.

"Well, she looks like the old Little Bit and acts like the old Little Bit, but where is the little troublemaker?"

Patti shook her head. "There's something going on here that we don't understand."

The very next day Miracle arrived all by himself. He didn't stay around long, but came back a second time that day. He seemed unsure and lonesome in his newly motherless condition.

Our questions were cleared up totally when Little Bit came back on the twenty-fifth, alone and happy to see us. She walked directly over to me, nuzzling my arm in her usual familiar way. It was obvious that she had abandoned Miracle, though usually mothers keep cubs alongside until mid-June. It was as if she couldn't wait to be footloose and cubless once

Little Bit looks over my shoulder after returning for
another summer.

more. That day Patti pronounced Little Bit as being "perfectly normal again." And little Miracle was now totally on his
own.

Perhaps the prospect of sex and mating had been part of
the equation in convincing Little Bit to dump Miracle early,
because it wasn't long before the first suitor came calling. On
May 26, a large male bear walked onto the front lawn, sniffed
the air, and then began literally, and deliberately, to stomp
around. He would raise each leg high, then plant it back down
hard, as if intentionally to leave deep footprints. If you've ever
seen the Lipizzaner stallions or a Tennessee walking horse,
you get the idea. The bear's walk had a sort of cadence or
rhythm to it.

Patti and I both caught the show, and while we were certainly impressed, we could not figure out the significance of this "dance." Later, we logically surmised that in sensing Little Bit was getting ready to mate, this big fellow had come courting and had managed to mark the turf in a way that wouldn't soon be forgotten.

This was one of the three or four largest male black bears we had ever seen, and he'd obviously been through the mating cycle a few times. Since we witnessed this ritual behavior only once, we figure very few people have seen it at all. We mentioned it to two or three people including Bill Peterson, the resident wildlife expert for the Department of Natural Resources, but no one seemed to know anything about it. Maybe the behavior was unique to that specific bear.

By Memorial Day, Little Bit had been back two and a half weeks, but there was no sign of Big Mama and her cubs. As always when one of our regulars went missing, we feared the worst.

At 10:30 P.M. on the evening of May 30, we heard a braying or squalling—at first faint, then gaining in intensity—out on the deck. I put down my book and went downstairs, thinking it was a typical bear argument over the seed box. The loud voice alone should have warned me it was Napoleon. Flipping on the outdoor light switch illuminated him on one side of the box and Honey on the other, pulling for all they were worth. And they were both in fine voice.

"Come back at last," I said, loud enough to rouse Patti. She raced downstairs, saw the cubs and said, "You guys had us scared to death something had happened to you."

When I opened the sliding glass door, the cubs forgot their squabbles and literally jumped into my arms. I had to contain them to keep them from running straight into the living room.

We celebrated their return, Big Mama as always waiting in the darkness near the steps, protecting the deck.

As we watched, we saw that compared to the lanky Miracle, these cubs were still quite small and thin. We supposed they had traveled a long way since emerging from their den. If bears could talk, what stories would they have told us?

The trio returned together the next day and then again on my birthday, June 2. By then, we knew the family split was imminent. In a matter of a few days, Big Mama would in fact abandon the yearlings and take another mate. As it turned out, she split them up the first week in June. Napoleon came back almost immediately. I remember his return vividly because he seemed lonely and stayed around a long time despite the heat of the sun on his still long and straggly winter coat.

That was also the day of the "honey episode." We had a nearly empty jar of Sue Bee Honey and thought it would be a real treat to give the newly orphaned cub a taste. We tipped the jar over the seeds, but the honey was thick and wouldn't pour, so Patti got a long-handled spoon and dug it out. Napoleon never hesitated. With his long tongue he reached for the dripping honey. Sitting like a little gentleman, he licked the spoon as often as Patti offered it to him.

His sister, on the other hand, seemed to simply vanish that summer. She came back one evening in midsummer, acted calm and polite, then ran off when a larger bear approached. That was the last we saw of her until the next year.

Meanwhile, Little Bit had been busy locating a suitable mate. When she returned in early June, her newfound mate came tagging along. And he was big, like close to 400 pounds big. He had a pair of small stripes on each side of his chest, which formed a pattern. So far, we had seen two other bears with distinctive white blazes or marks on their chests. The

Little Bit and a very large stranger who followed her
home one day.

first was Grandfather, whose mark was a white splotch. Then there was Sarge, with his three stripes.

As Little Bit came up on the deck, her new mate waited below. He was patient, which was fortunate, because she was in no hurry. She got up on the bench, sat down with her stubby legs hanging over the edge, and began to eat seeds that had been left on the railing for the birds. She always sat this way, like a person instead of a bear, and sometimes she would remain seated for an hour or more. This was one of those times. I looked down to see if her boyfriend was still waiting.

"Still there?" Patti asked.

"Still there," I replied. We checked this three times in about an hour.

"Still there?"

"Still there."

Finally, the pair left and we saw no more of Little Bit for several days. When she returned, a different suitor accompanied her. This bear was solid black and only a bit larger than she was. He also waited patiently while she ate and seemed to have no interest in his own hunger.

In many species of animals during mating season, males hold combat over breeding rights. This was something we knew occurred among moose and deer but never saw among bears. The male bears seemed rather laid back about mating, and we learned they actually forego their search for food during the season.

Finally, Big Mama came back with a boyfriend. He also waited below, just out of sight. I tried looking from various vantage points and finally got a glimpse.

"Oh no," I groaned.

"What is it. What's wrong?" Patti asked in a worried voice.

"I can't believe it," I continued.

"What is it?" She was more insistent now.

"Big Mama's boyfriend is the same one that Little Bit had. You know, the one with the white marks."

"So what's wrong with that?" She asked after brief thought. "They're not like people."

"I know, but it seems wrong somehow."

I'm sure it's ridiculous to think bears should follow rules similar to humans', but somehow, after spending so much time with Little Bit, she no longer seemed to be a wild bear. It took my brain a minute to sort things out. Finally, I laughed. "Hey, it's okay with me. This old guy is probably the prize of the forest. More power to him."

As I mentioned, we kept track of bear activity in those days by writing in a daily journal.

Here is Patti's entry from Saturday, July 8:

I woke up and looked out the one living room window that had no curtain. There was Scar sitting up, looking in the window and quietly waiting to be noticed. He sat unmoving and seemed content to just sit on his fanny and beg like a big black dog. I opened the curtain to find Little Bit hovering right by the door. She had been sleeping in something that stuck to her head like a lacy scarf. Scar's muzzle also was suspiciously light-colored. What have they been up to?

When I looked down the driveway, I saw a trail of garbage. They had opened the garage door, pushing it up a good six feet. The garbage was strewn in a trail out the door, down the drive, then around the house. Meanwhile Toby had joined the other two on the deck. Little Bit and Scar looked at me with solemn faces, like two mischievous kids. Jack ran the two boys off the deck, and they circled the house, awaiting their chance to come back up.

One morning that month, we found the garage door up and garbage strewn everywhere across the side yard and driveway. We started to watch closely whenever any bear went near the garage. Sure enough, the culprit was quickly discovered. It was Little Bit showing off for her boyfriend. The garage door was of heavy, solid-wood construction. It took some strength to lift. However, Little Bit made child's play of the effort.

When I was in school, we were taught that the difference between man and the animals was that man could reason. I assure you, however, that Little Bit could reason. She may have seen me lift the door, but she still had to learn the mechanics of it. I had been especially concerned that a bear might lift the door and get trapped inside the garage. That could lead to a hysterical bear and a heart-stopping surprise for anyone (me or Patti) when they went inside to get the car. Fortunately, Little Bit learned to lift the door at least six feet, which kept it from sliding back down.

I had been contemplating the purchase of an automatic door opener for some time, and this seemed the perfect time to try one out. That week, Patti and I went to Duluth and bought one at Sears. Surprisingly, I installed it myself correctly. And that put an end to Little Bit's latest shenanigans.

The garage also turned out to be the site of our annual company fish fry that summer. Usually the event was held on the beach east of Grand Marais, where we would cook fresh salmon and lake trout over an open fire. Every year it rained, however, and we'd end up spending part of the fish fry waiting in our cars for the rain to stop.

This year, we decided to have the party down behind the house near the river, where there was already a fire pit. In case of rain, everyone could take shelter in the house. The day of the picnic, the weather was true to form. It rained. Prepared for the worst, this year we set up tables in the garage and also on the driveway under a big tarp. Not very scenic, but workable.

"Where are the bears?" someone asked.

I explained they were shy and didn't come on cue. It began to rain harder, so we took our plates inside to eat in the living room. Sure enough, as soon as everyone was seated, Little Bit arrived on the back deck and peered inside. Dinner was instantly forgotten, and about a dozen noses pressed themselves against the glass. Flashbulbs flared. Scared by all the attention, Little Bit retreated in confusion.

The rain ended, and everyone went outside to roast marshmallows on the grill. After a few minutes, one of the little boys pointed across the front lawn and said, "There's a bear." He'd spotted Little Bit peeking around the corner of the house, just behind the pin cherry tree, wondering what was going on.

"If you go over there for a closer look, she'll run away," I said. "Pretend you're not interested and she might stay."

I needn't have worried that the child would frighten Little Bit. He peered at the cautious bear from behind his father's legs.

As dusk fell, people started leaving for home and, spooked by the slamming of car doors, Little Bit again retreated into the woods. When they were gone, however, her curiosity brought her back once more. This time, seeing only Patti and me, she came right over. We were cleaning up and putting chairs away in the garage when I noticed her following me, sniffing around as we bustled about. She was acting like a great big black dog, in no apparent hurry, not bothering the garbage, just following closely on my heels wherever I went.

Patti came into the garage and gave me a quizzical look. "Everything okay?" she asked.

"Oh yes, just me and Rover here," I replied, pointing to the bear, who was sniffing around in a corner. As long as I stayed occupied with picking up and putting away, Little Bit was content to follow me around the garage. She didn't appear hungry, but simply wanted company.

She had been walking around all day through the dripping rain-soaked bushes, but when I touched her coat that evening, the fur deep down and closest to her skin was perfectly dry. That's because her fur grew in each summer in two lengths. First came a very soft, dense, short coat, followed by a thick, coarse long coat. The result was a nice waterproofing job.

Even though their coats protect them from getting wet, bears shed water by giving themselves a good shake, like a dog. The water flies in all directions. Little Bit waited until Patti and I were both within range before she shook herself. "Gee, thanks, Little Bit," we said.

When I told a friend that we sometimes spent three or four hours outside with Little Bit every day, he wondered aloud what we did during all that time. As I told him, sometimes we didn't do much of anything except sit outside with her. Patti would sit down on the deck floor and Little Bit would deposit herself next to her, leaning slightly against her shoulder. With no cub to worry about, she had become very mellow and relaxed. She would sometimes climb the steps to the deck, get up on the bench, and simply sit there, looking out at the creek and the forest.

One Sunday, we came home from church to find her sitting at her customary post. As the wind began to blow, however, she got uneasy and began to pace. Patti and I sprayed ourselves with Deep Woods Off and went outside to sit with

Me and Little Bit, just hanging out.

her. She immediately relaxed and climbed up on the bench,
where we all sat for over an hour, Patti and I reading the
Sunday paper and Little Bit eating a few seeds while she gazed
out over her domain.

That evening, about an hour after supper, Little Bit was
looking in the window to see if we were home. The wind had
quieted down and a horde of mosquitoes followed her every
move. She paid them no heed, but their presence was a warning to Patti and me that we'd best douse ourselves liberally
with bug spray before joining her.

Minnesotans often joke about how the mosquito is the
state bird. How mosquitoes are big, bloodthirsty, and plentiful. How, amassed in a dark cloud, they follow the bears
around, fending off any creature that ventures near.

That night, we stayed outside for more than two hours

until, at about 10:30, the light slipped away to the west. I had my bear stick near in case any rowdies or long noses chose to join us, while Patti had donned her wide-brim anti-bat hat.

As night decended, so did the flying squirrels, to dine on sunflower seeds. Flyers, as they are called for short, have huge eyes for night vision and the softest fur of any animal I know. Normally they are shy and nervous, but after landing next to us as they came and went, they became surprisingly calm in our company. To reach the deck, the flyers would climb a nearby tree, from which they would spring toward the railing. After downing a few mouthfuls of seeds they would soar from the deck, down the hill, and land low on a tree trunk. Then they'd climb up and repeat the process.

To fly as they do through the air, squirrels have flaps or membranes that connect their front and back legs, similar to the webbing on a duck's foot. When they take flight, they spread their legs to stretch their "wings." In this way they can glide fifty to seventy-five feet through the air.

We sat with Little Bit, watching as the squirrels' dim shapes soared from the trees and landed near us. They would run through the seeds in front of Little Bit and she would ignore them. Then they would fly back to a tree down by the creek. Their aim was impeccable; they never missed.

That evening, we were able to pet them for the first time. We sat quietly as they climbed into the seed box. Then we'd move our hands very slowly and stroke them gently with a single finger on their backs. Very fragile, they're apparently easy to catch by predators, such as owls or pine martens.

These flying squirrels were among the most gentle and unusual creatures we met in our years on Elbow Creek. Often, they would share the seed box with Little Bit or one of the cubs. Little Bit would ignore the squirrels, but the cubs turned the encounters into games of hide and seek.

That night, when Patti and I finally got up to go inside and escape the bugs, Little Bit also got up to leave. She had not stayed for the seeds or the flyers, she had been there because we were there.

The previous summer, when we had built the seven-foot-high cedar fence, the Shepherd Sisters had been only half-grown and weighed no more than thirty-five pounds. Now they were full-grown, with Sheba weighing eighty-five pounds and Shadow seventy-five.

If any animal could upset Little Bit, it was Sheba, who patrolled the inner fence line, barking at the bears. Somehow, she had determined that bears were her mortal enemy. Her self-appointed job was to warn us of their arrivals and then chase them away. Shadow, on the other hand, had no interest and simply watched from the sidelines.

That spring, Sheba took up the job of protecting the house from bears. I swear, she could smell them right through a wall or a closed window. Unlike us, she was never surprised by them. The regulars soon figured out that she was on one side of the fence and they were on the other, but her barking would make them agitated. Little Bit and Big Mama, especially, took to swatting the fence. To quiet the dog, we put her downstairs. The dogs had soft beds in the basement and slept there at night. Somehow, Sheba considered herself off duty when downstairs. No matter how many bears might be tromping around on the deck, she would remain silent.

About the middle of summer, a terrific ruckus broke out back at the corner of the fence where the old bear trail emerged from the woods. Sheba was barking madly, and a bear could be heard swatting the rough-sawn boards.

I went outside on the deck and looked down the fence line. A bear was sitting relaxed under the tree at the far end. It was

Scar, back for the first time all summer. I watched him sit there calmly while the dog, hair standing on end along her shoulders and back, barked and raged out of his sight on the other side of the fence. Finally, Sheba would tire of her efforts and stop to determine whether she had succeeded in driving off the bear. Then Scar would lean forward, cuff the boards, and rake his claws along the wood.

Off she would go again, barking angrily as Scar sat back to enjoy the show. They repeated the sequence twice as I watched. Then Scar tired of his fun and came up on the deck. I swear he had a mischievous little smile on his face. I shook my head, then went around and put Sheba inside before her voice gave out. "They're teasing with you, Sheba. Don't you know that? Maybe you should quit barking so much and listen more. Then you'd figure out what was happening on the other side."

The dog was no fool. By the end of that summer, she'd learned to do exactly as I suggested. She would run the fence line, using her nose to pinpoint the bear's location, then listen. As the fence boards dried out, small cracks opened up between them, so dog and bear could also get glimpses of each other. Sheba became the silent hunter instead of the barking aggressor. It made life more tolerable for all of us, and certainly quieter.

Because Little Bit was an almost daily visitor, Sheba quit paying any attention to her toward the end of summer. I'm sure she knew that bear's particular scent and realized that when she arrived, she'd probably stay awhile.

Scar stayed off and on until August, when he left again. We suspected that the early part of summer had been spent charming girl bears and the month of August would be devoted to the berry patches. Scar, now five years old, was no longer the homebody he used to be.

* * *

After mid-June, the summer of '94 began to dry out and heat up. Bushes that had heralded an excellent crop of blueberries produced a scant harvest. Every now and again, you could smell the smoke from a forest fire burning up near Ely, about eighty miles northwest as the crow flies.

Old-timers always used to say that summer starts to go downhill, feeling more like fall, and the nights cool off after Fisherman's Picnic, an August celebration held in Grand Marais. That year, the weather was dry and warm right on through the month and well into September.

Water in the creek was low, with many rocks showing. The swimming hole down in front of our house was hardly deep enough to be inviting for a bear. But Little Bit discovered an even better swimming hole about a half-mile south, in the Devil's Track River near Ed Hedstrom's house. Patti learned of the find when she ran into Ed's wife at the grocery store.

"We've been seeing your bear, Little Bit, swimming in the river," she said. "There's a nice swimming hole where all the Hedstrom kids have gone to play for years. Our kids swim there now, and Little Bit has found it. I can see her from the bridge."

The Hedstroms didn't mind sharing their swimming hole with Little Bit, who was becoming well known locally. In the evening, after a hot day, she'd arrive at the back deck with ferns clinging to her wet coat. From her bedraggled appearance, we deduced she had been for a swim, then had taken a nap in the cool, shady ferns. For a large bear with a heavy fur coat, that was about the only way to keep cool on a hot afternoon.

I suppose the heat also played a part in my decision that summer to quit walking behind my old lawn mower and start riding one instead. My dream of owning a John Deere lawn tractor was no sooner fulfilled than the guilt began. I had spent too much money. I didn't need such a big mower for such a small lawn. I didn't deserve to ride. In such a case, you do what you can to alleviate the guilt. My solution was to add a lot more grass to mow, which would then justify the mower.

Patti and I had talked about clearing the area between the house and the creek, which was now so overgrown we could hardly see any water. So we called Tim Mathison, a contractor who was married to my cousin Joan. I outlined my ideas for clearing and smoothing an area 100 feet by 250 feet, leaving only about ten trees, which we marked with ribbons. It took two days, using a large bulldozer, to remove the trees and generally level the ground. The job was finished on a Friday, and Tim came by that evening to pick up his bulldozer.

I had gone to a meeting and Patti was lazing outside on the back deck with Little Bit. Suddenly, she heard someone calling. "Hi up there." It was Tim, walking across the open area. He had looked up and seen Patti and a huge bear about three times as big as she was. She waved back.

"Is that bear Little Bit?" he asked.

She nodded in the affirmative. "Pretty big bear," he said. "You out there alone with it?" Again, she nodded. Little Bit, however, was getting nervous. She shifted her enormous bulk, trying to hide behind Patti's 120-pound frame.

Tim started up the dozer and it clattered over the shale and rocks, causing Little Bit to try to shrink enough to become completely hidden. She had accepted the changed landscape surprisingly well, but the noisy dozer scared her badly.

What had been a thick forest, criss-crossed by bear tunnels, was now an open plain covered by rocks. We wondered what the other bears would make of it. We wouldn't have to wait long to find out. That same evening a young male came out of the woods, nose to the ground, and walked nearly halfway across the opening before looking up to discover what had happened. He did a double take, then spun around and ran back to the safety of the forest. He was one confused bear.

After realizing that our open area was about 95 percent rocks and 5 percent dirt, we had Tim bring in twenty-five loads of dirt and spread it around. We planted grass September 1 and covered the seeds with straw just in time to benefit from a wonderful soaking rain. The weather stayed warm, and by mid-September we had a beautiful field of bright new green growing through the straw.

To our amazement, the chaos we thought would occur when the bears spotted the open field never materialized. They ventured out carefully, but were soon playing recklessly in the grass. We put out corn in one corner of the newly sown back lawn and immediately had takers of all kinds. A flock of mallards swooped in and decided to stay until everything froze up in November. Our small deer herd found the corn, and soon they were racing about. They frolicked there until the snow covered the ground, and lingered beyond that. This gorgeous wild life was an unexpected bonus.

And all this because of a lawn tractor.

7

A WALK IN THE
WOODS WITH A BEAR

It was just a walk in the woods, but a special one, because my companion was Little Bit. Nearing hibernation, she had grown heavy and slow through the golden days of September.

That day after lunch, she had arrived at the house with her nose covered with dirt. "Looks like she's been working on her den," Patti said. "This might be a good time to see if she'll take us along."

Patti had been struggling to get her erratic blood pressure under control, so I talked her out of what might be a tough hike through rough terrain. But when Little Bit left later in the afternoon after a long visit, I was close behind. Down across the new lawn we ambled, crossing the creek on stepping stones. On the other side, in deep shadows, was a steep hill where assorted trees clung to life in rocky crevices.

It was a hard climb for me, clutching first at a rock, then a tree trunk, then another rock. Little Bit went up like a mountain goat and was soon over the crest and out of sight. Puffing hard, I reached the crest and looked ahead into the low sun glinting through heavy underbrush. Nothing appeared to be moving. Had I lost her already?

I started along what appeared to be a faint path through deep grass. Suddenly, there she was right ahead, standing silently in the shade, looking back at me. "Can I tag along, Little Bit?" I asked. "I won't get in your way or anything."

She turned away and started down the trail, which soon led out onto a more open meadow covered with grasses and low bushes. She stopped to nibble a particular vine, then pulled a long string of leaves loose and chewed on them. I waited about twenty feet behind, trying to be inconspicuous but failing, since Little Bit insisted on looking back at me while whe nibbled.

We went on again across the meadow and through the forest to the west. The pace was slow and easy for her, but I had to work to keep up as we went over deadfalls and around stumps.

It was a perfect day, crisp as a newly picked apple, the sunlight brightening leaves that were already turning gold. What an improbable adventure, I thought, to be walking with a wild bear through its domain.

Ahead of us was what appeared to be an impenetrable thicket of alders and moose willow. Little Bit disappeared into it and I tried to watch where she had gone. I could see nothing until I hunkered down and peered beneath the thick foliage. Then what looked like a narrow tunnel appeared. At first I was surprised she had made it through such a low and narrow place, but she was nowhere to be seen. I stood up, perplexed, and decided I would have to go around the tunnel and hope to meet her on ahead. The ground was wet as I struggled through the interlocking brush. I did not know where she was, but she would have had no trouble locating me from the crashing and banging I was making as I rearranged the forest.

I've lost her for good, I thought. The noise alone will scare her off. I came out of the dense underbrush and cut back toward the tunnel, looking for some sign of a trail. I'd spent many years studying deer trails, but bear trails were different. They're either superhighways or virtually invisible.

After walking about fifty yards, I stood quietly, hoping for a glimpse of black fur or a sound of some kind. Nothing. A bee droned on its way past me, and some frogs started calling in the distance. Well, it was fun while it lasted, I thought, deciding to go a hundred yards farther west in the one last hope of picking her up again.

To my utter shock, I nearly walked into her before I saw her standing there, in my path, eating apple-like things from a bush while glancing back at my approach. I don't know if she was waiting for me or if she just happened to find a favored food in a convenient place, but there she was.

Shading my eyes against the sun sliding toward the west, I watched Little Bit pluck the fruit with her lips, then start off again. We went into a glade of old-growth white pine, some three or four feet in diameter. It was only a small area, but felt like a great, gloomy cathedral. Little Bit and I walked in silence across the shadowed forest floor with its thick blanket of needles. We had come a mile or more, and I wondered where she was leading me.

As we came out from under the canopy of tall pines, the bear stopped to sniff the light breeze. Then she made a right turn to the north and set off at a steady pace. I fell further behind as we went, but kept her in sight. She stopped up ahead on a hillside and I stopped as well, needing a breather.

She seemed to be looking off to her left. Then I saw what she was watching. It was another bear, virtually identical in size, walking toward her. As I was downwind and perhaps forty yards away, the other bear was not aware of me. He moved steadily toward her, and when he came up to her they seemed to touch noses.

Little Bit looked back down the hill and the other bear followed her gaze. Though bears have notoriously bad eyes, Little Bit's companion detected something unnatural in my outline and blew air loudly from his nostrils. This seemed to upset Little Bit, who quickly stepped away from him. He huffed and puffed at my silent form, then got more agitated and trotted up the hill, stopping once for another good look before disappearing over the top.

I looked back and Little Bit was gone. In the time I'd been watching the other bear leave, she had slipped away. Going up the hill, I felt sure I'd see her any moment. How could a large, slow-moving bear just disappear? But she had. I got to the knob of the hill and looked in all directions. Nothing. Neither bear was visible.

I turned off toward the northeast. It seemed the logical direction she had gone, but there was no sign of her, no sound. I shook my head in bewilderment, then set about the job of getting back home. It took another hour to travel cross-country to the river, then back down the river to our house, where supper was waiting and I told my story to Patti.

We had no sooner sat down to eat than a familiar face peeked in the sliding glass door. "Where have you been, you turkey?" I asked aloud in frustration. It's a wonder Little Bit hadn't beaten me back home.

The next morning Patti washed several loads of clothes and hung them outside. It promised to be another glorious and sunny day. A while later, she noticed that two of the cats, Caesar and Einstein, were sitting on the dining room table, looking out the window in the direction of the clothesline.

At first she paid no attention. Then, seeing that the cats

continued to sit there watching, she glanced out. "I don't see anything," she said to them. "What are you guys watching so intently?"

At noon, she went out to check the clothes and bring in those that were dry. As she started to work, she noticed a gap on the line where something was obviously missing. She thought about it briefly, then it hit her. The pink bathrobe was gone. It was thick and comfy. Her favorite.

The clothesline was near the woods, so she walked over and looked around. Then she came inside and called for me to come out. "Someone has taken my pink bathrobe, and I intend it find it. You go that way, and I'll try over here."

We split up and I went into the woods, where I looked for several minutes before giving up and returning to the lawn. Moments later, Patti emerged on the other side of the yard, carrying her bathrobe. "I'm gonna spank that bear," she said, explaining that someone had pulled the bathrobe down, carried it into the woods, then used it to soften a daybed in the tall grass. Whoever had used it had left a small whorl of black fur as evidence.

"Any other damage to it?" I asked.

"No, I guess I'm lucky it's still in one piece."

She took the bathrobe inside and rewashed it. When she hung it up, she anchored it to the line with four clothespins. Twice in the next hour she checked it. Twice it was still there. The third time it was still there, and the fourth. Maybe, she thought, the idea of using her bathrobe as a bed liner had been forgotten.

A while later, she went out to bring in the last of the wash, which should by now be dry. The bathrobe was gone. "Oh no, not again," she wailed.

With several of the windows open, I heard her clearly and hustled outside in time to see her striding straight for the spot where the daybeds were located. This time, she caught the culprit red-handed.

"Shame on you, Little Bit. That's my bathrobe, not yours," she said. By now Little Bit was up and retreating from her pink-lined bed.

I met Patti emerging with bathrobe again in hand. "Little Bit?" I asked.

She nodded. "Who else? At least she didn't seem to harm it any." After being washed for the third time that day, the furry robe—found to be still in good condition—was tumbled dry in the basement dryer.

That same evening, we were outside on the deck feeding chipmunks. Our friend Chester was there, squabbling with his cousins while filling his cheeks with nuts. Little Bit arrived and climbed ponderously up the stairs to the deck. She strode straight through the swirl of chipmunks, paying no attention, and went right over to Patti, who gathered a small pile of almonds for her on the bench.

Little Bit ignored the nuts and nuzzled Patti's hand, as she often did when she wanted to be hand-fed. Sometimes she absolutely would not eat them in any other way. This was one of those days.

Patti picked up the nuts she had placed on the bench. Because of very low blood pressure, she'd become dizzy and her hand was shaking. Little Bit saw her hand trembling and did something totally unexpected. She lifted her large paw, cupped it beneath Patti's hand, and actually held her hand steady while gently picking the nuts up with her mouth.

Patti said nothing, but she understood, and her eyes filled with tears. She stroked the big bear's neck and turned away. It was a special moment, one that we could never have predicted and that we would never forget.

* * *

Little Bit helps to steady Patti's hand.

Chester was one of a band of a dozen or more chipmunks who had taken up residence on and below our back deck. In the fall, they went into feeding frenzies, fighting each other over sunflower seeds and anything else we might put out.

Patti said they reminded her of bumper cars at a carnival, careening off in all directions. They'd run off the edge of the deck, fall ten feet, get up, dust themselves off, and climb right back into the battle. Sometimes they seemed indestructible.

Chester was accustomed to racing in front of us and standing up on his little hind legs to beg. One day, he got confused and decided Little Bit might also give him nuts if he begged from her. He stood in front of her. She ignored him. He climbed her furry front leg. She gave a shake and he fell off. He persisted in begging until she got annoyed. Finally, Little Bit took a paw and went "splat" on the deck. The only part of Chester showing beneath her claws was his stubby tail. We thought for certain it was all over for him. Curtains. But when Little Bit raised her paw, Chester popped up like a Jack-in-the-box and scurried away. He wasn't even hurt.

My walk with Little Bit made us determined to find at least one den that fall. We figured the hills and cliffs on both sides of the creek held the most promise, so we concentrated our efforts there. One Sunday, we spent all afternoon tramping around looking for dens. We found daybeds along the creek and a few signs of bear activity, but nothing resembling a den, even though we looked into every crevice and under every piece of deadfall. Our earlier thoughts returned; these bears could be hibernating several miles from our house, in which case there's no way we'd ever find them. For the first time, I wished we had some kind of tracking device to locate them inside their dens.

Most everyone thinks that bears den in caves or beneath the roots of old trees. That's not always the way it happens. Sometimes, they crawl into brush piles or under deadfalls. On occasion, they prefer sleeping accommodations right out in the open. Researchers say a big bear gives off so much heat, it can't sleep comfortably while enclosed in a cave or other type of shelter. Therefore, it just lies down on the ground and goes to sleep. Ultimately, it is covered by the snow. Its body heat melts the snow next to it, creating a snow cave.

Having no cubs to jostle them awake every time they got tired, both Little Bit and Big Mama had gone to their dens by September 22. People not familiar with bears couldn't believe they were already asleep. "But it's still nice out. There's no snow," they'd say.

There is an old Minnesota wives' tale, widely believed, that bears do not den until the first good snowfall, when the snow will cover their tracks and they will be safe. It sounded good to me. Very logical. I believed it when I heard it and even explained it to Patti.

Apparently, the folks at the state capitol also believed it. When they scheduled the first bear-hunting season, they set the opening day as September 15. That year, most of the bears had already denned by then, so the season was a failure. It took the bureaucrats quite some time to sort out what had happened and move the season back to September 1.

That month, when the bears went into hibernation, we ran a color photo of Little Bit and me sitting together on our deck. The photo, which had been taken by Patti, was entitled "Conversation with a Bear." You would have thought we'd run a photo of Bigfoot. People started calling right away, wondering if they could buy a print of the photo. People were simply amazed at the shot and wanted to show it to their friends. A few wondered if the bear was tame or if the photo was doctored in any way.

That photo also convinced a number of former skeptics that we really did have some experience around bears. "Gee, that was some picture," one of my uncles said a couple of weeks later. "I knew you had those bears around, but I never knew you'd get that close." I smiled. If he could see Patti hugging Little Bit or playing with Big Mama's cubs, he'd really be in shock.

After the photo appeared, a number of readers came in and told us their bear stories. One lady said she didn't want anybody to know, but she had been feeding an orphaned yearling up at Poplar Lake all summer. "We'd never tell anybody else," she revealed in a voice just above a whisper, "but we knew you'd understand."

We heard three or four similar stories, followed by worries that something terrible must have happened in late September. The young bears just seemed to have vanished.

The famous "Conversation with a Bear" photo that we ran
in the newspaper.

We would explain that the bears by then were probably
ready to hibernate. "So early?" They'd ask.

Oh yes, we'd assure them. Well-fed bears den quite early,
certainly in late September. Only a few last until October.

One lady called us from Finland, Minnesota, a little com-
munity about sixty miles west. She'd heard we knew about

bears and wondered if we could come and pick up a yearling that had been hanging around her house for a couple of weeks. She was worried he wouldn't make it through the winter.

"Are you giving him anything to eat?"

"I would if I knew what to give him," she said. "But you'd know better what to do."

I told her about sunflower seeds and wished her well, explaining we had no way to transport a lively yearling bear. I also assured her that a healthy, well-fed yearling would probably get through the winter just fine without any special help from us.

8

A BELATED
HOMECOMING—
SPRING 1995

In the spring of 1995, anticipation simmered among county residents for the return of the bears. As the snow melted along Lake Superior in mid-April, people we saw threw question after question at us about Little Bit. Is she back yet? Will she have cubs? When will she be back? Can we come up and see her?

To those and other signs of interest, Patti and I would respond like proud grandparents, whipping out photos and telling stories. There were times when I had to shake my head and remind myself that we were running a newspaper and not a bear information center.

We waited a long time for the bears that spring. The snow was gone in the woods by the end of April. The ice vanished from the lakes. Fishing opener came and went. The ducks battled over the corn. Mid-May arrived and there was still no sign of any bears.

Our worries were amplified by well-meaning bear enthu-siasts who kept dropping in. What? They're not back? Do you think they've been killed? Maybe they didn't survive the win-ter? What could have happened? Obviously, we didn't know what, if anything, had happened. So we held our breath and prayed for their safety and hoped to see them soon.

Memorial Day slid by, and one evening, I went into the living room to find Patti sitting alone, looking out the window, tears in her eyes. "I'm sorry," she said. "I just don't know what to do. What if they don't come back? What if something has happened?"

"We don't know if anything is wrong." I said. "Our fears are just getting to us. They've been this late before. It's noth-ing to worry about yet." I was trying to calm her feelings, but I had the same uneasiness. These were wild animals. There were many dangers out there, not the least of which were the guns I'd heard being fired just about every day.

"Give it a few more days," I suggested. "Then if they don't show up, we'll go out and start asking around." She nodded in agreement and wiped her eyes.

We waited. Every sound would send us running to the back door for a look outside. Every time I walked from room to room, I'd check the driveway and front yard. Fortunately, there was also office work for us to do. The end of the month was always busiest for Patti, and the paper grew in page count as we passed from Memorial Day into the summer vacation season.

Then on the night of May 29, after we had turned out the lights and gone to bed, we heard a faint noise coming from outside, around the back of the house. "What is that?" I asked. Patti answered by throwing back the covers and getting up. I was right behind her. What we were hearing was a cub with laryngitis squalling from a treetop. We hurried downstairs and, sure enough, there was Big Mama, cross-eyed and flat-nosed, standing alone on the deck. We stepped out to put more seeds in the empty box and she settled down to eat. The cub was now silent.

"Is that your cub up the tree?" Patti asked the bear. Big Mama looked at her and then up the tree, almost as if she understood. We shined the flashlight up the old white spruce, but could not see the tiny cub. We thought at the time it was alone. Although we stayed up a couple of hours more in case the hoarse cub came onto the deck, nothing happened. Big Mama went quietly on her way.

The next night, Big Mama was back with her froggy-voiced cub. This time, as we turned on the lights to illuminate the back deck, we saw the cub scamper away into the darkness. We opened the door to greet Big Mama and heard the cub climbing a nearby tree. Later, after we had gone to bed, the cub started squalling in its hoarse voice again. It didn't last long, though, and soon we drifted off to sleep.

At the office, the next day, a subscriber came in and asked if Little Bit had come back yet. We said no, and he told us he'd seen a large mother bear walking alongside a back road with two cubs. He said they were heading in the direction of our house, not more than a couple of miles away. Somehow, I didn't attribute much credibility to his story. It could have been any female bear, not necessarily Little Bit. What would a shy bear like her be doing along a public road? It didn't make sense to either of us.

That night, a male bear visited briefly, but that was it. Still no sign of Little Bit. Our nerves were about shot from all the false alarms. The male bear came back the following night, but by now we hadn't even seen Big Mama or her hoarse cub for two nights. Had he gotten sick and died? We were obviously at wit's end. Here it was June 1 and no Little Bit.

"Give it another day or two," I suggested. Though I preached patience, I was out of it myself.

There was a creak on the deck, then another. "Sounds like we've got a visitor," I said.

"Probably that young male bear coming back," Patti responded.

I put my nose back in the book, but then heard what could have been a paw against the back glass door. "Oh well, I better go have a look." I said. I went downstairs, flipped on the deck light, and rolled up the wood curtain. "Oh, my God," I said loudly. As I heard Patti's feet hit the floor upstairs, I stood looking at Little Bit and two leggy little cubs. What a happy moment. Patti bounded down the stairs. "She's back with two cubs," I laughed.

"Thank you, Lord," she said and went straight into the kitchen, where she fixed a bucket of milk.

I opened the door, and Patti set out the milk and a handful of almonds. Little Bit leaned forward and slurped up milk

Little Bit and her new cubs cross the freshly planted yard.

while her cubs nuzzled close to her, wondering no doubt what kind of creatures we were.

Little Bit made a motion as if to get up, and the two little black cubs scurried across the deck, down the steps, and fled up the old white spruce. She watched them go, then sat down and gorged herself on milk, sunflower seeds, and almonds.

"What a sight for sore eyes," I said, in my excitement.

"Wow, did you see the way they minded her," Patti marveled. "She handles these cubs like she's really in charge."

It's hard to describe just how pleased we both felt at seeing Little Bit again. She looked very healthy, not much thinner than she had been eight months earlier, when we had last seen her. She acted totally relaxed. Her two furry bundles minded her and followed right on her heels. Such a wonderful change from the days of Miracle two summers earlier.

All our first impressions were reinforced early the next morning at 5:15 A.M., when she returned to the back deck.

Patti heard the familiar tap of Little Bit's paw on the glass door and jumped up out of bed. The bear was alone, having put the two cubs up a nearby tree. She seemed to want equal amounts of food and affection. It was just like old times. The only cause of concern was her new route when leaving. She had always gone into the woods out back or across the river. Now she was leaving by way of the driveway, which led to the busy Gunflint Trail.

We decided that the man's report of seeing her along a back road was probably true. But why had she suddenly taken to walking along roads? Cars had always frightened her. Had she lost her fear of them? Why did our bears always do the unexpected?

The real surprise still lay ahead. It would leave us shaking our heads and trying to fit answers to our many questions for a long time, until we finally just accepted it as another bear mystery. That night, on my birthday, Big Mama came back with a special gift. We heard her on the deck at 9:45 P.M. and when we lit up the place, we saw she was alone. We did not hear the hoarse little cub she'd had earlier, and we immediately feared it had probably been sick and died.

We watched Big Mama settle down and munch seeds for a couple of minutes, then we went into the family room to watch TV. At a commercial, I went back toward the kitchen for an iced-tea refill. On the way, I glanced out to see if she was still there. She was sitting, looking down, and I followed her gaze. Then I stopped in my tracks. Swirling around her feet were not one, not two, but three little tiny black cubs.

"Holy mackerel," I said, more out of shock than anything else. "Patti, get in here."

"You won't believe this," I said, as she rounded the corner into the living room. I was pointing at the door.

She looked out through the glass, registered the scene before her, then opened the door and asked, "Big Mama, are all these cubs yours? Where have all of you been hiding?" I guess she wanted some answers and decided to go straight to the source. But of course they weren't talking. They were too busy scampering, rolling, climbing, and hiding.

I just stood there with my mouth open, not really comprehending how Big Mama had managed to go from one froggy-voiced cub to three silent ones. After about five minutes, during which a couple of the cubs had sampled the seeds, she led the babies down to the old white spruce, shooed them up the trunk, then returned to pass some more time on the deck. She had acted nervous with the cubs around, but now she was relaxed enough to lie down and fold her front paws underneath her as all bears do when comfortable eating.

Patti looked at me. "You're sure this is Big Mama?"

I nodded. "Same bear as we had here with the loud cub."

"So where's the loud cub? And where did she get these three?"

I shook my head, not having any idea what had happened. All I knew was that inexplicably she had three silent, skinny little black cubs with distinctive ear tufts. The cubs stayed up the old spruce for about fifteen minutes, until called down by their mother's throaty "clunks" as she was leaving. Silently, the group went off into the dark forest.

After Big Mama and her brood left, we talked about the mystery of the cubs and hypothesized some answers. Theory Number One was that she'd had three cubs all along, but had tried to leave them all up in a tree before coming to the deck. One of the three, being sick or insecure, had insisted on staying close to her. Theory Number Two was that she had given birth to four cubs, one of which caught a cold. It had died and the other three had survived to join her on the deck the night of June 2.

Either of these theories might have been the answer to the mystery, because we had experienced a period of cold rain a couple of weeks earlier, just the kind of weather that might make a very small cub sick. But of course, we can never know the truth. For now, we were just happy to see her with three healthy little cubs.

The next ten days were a time of acquainting ourselves with Little Bit's cubs and letting them experience us. She made it easy. She visited from two to four times per day for the entire period. Some days were really just one long visit interrupted only by naps and nursing the cubs.

We started by sitting outside and watching them. This established the basic fact that one was a boy, the other a girl. Three more days passed, and Patti hit upon names we felt were fun and easy to remember. The boy became Winnie,

Winnie and Pooh during an early-season ice storm.

while the girl was Pooh. Within about six weeks, they would know and respond to these names, as would Little Bit. When called by name, she would usually come to us. The cubs followed her lead, but would turn their heads when their names were called.

At their age and size, the cubs resembled agile monkeys. That they would grow up to be large bears required a real stretch of the imagination. Up in the old white spruce, where they spent a part of each day, they were fearless acrobats, swinging from the limbs, "wirewalking" the thin uneven surfaces, snoozing in unprotected positions.

It soon became obvious that Winnie was the larger and more ambitious cub, eager to try new things and more confident when close to us. Pooh held back with more caution and studied her options. This was typical of every pair of cubs we watched. The male was the larger and more dominant.

It had not rained in two weeks, and the garden, such as it was, looked parched. I purchased two new hoses to stretch from the house to the garden plot two hundred feet away and started sprinkling. Little Bit liked to take her cubs up to a shady area next to the garden, where she would play with them and let them nurse. The day I bought the hose, she shooed them under the old shed for their naps while she stood guard beside it. But tiring of her perch, she soon discovered the fun of playing with the hose. Every time she bit a little hole in it, she got a taste of icy water. Before long she had turned the new hose into a sieve and had gotten herself wetter than the garden.

That afternoon, when I went up to change the location of the sprinkler, I noticed there was very little water pressure. At first, I thought there was a crimp in the hose, but when I checked it, I got soaked. I looked at Little Bit, who sneaked over into the woods behind a bush. There she could peek out without being seen, or so she thought. I have no doubt she knew that she'd been naughty.

I rerigged the hose setup, using a couple of old hoses and the new one that was still intact. Then I waited until she was gone to turn on the water. An hour later, she was up there with the hose in her mouth, once more having a fine time.

Without hoses, the garden had to put up quite a struggle on its own. The drought continued, and it would be accurate to

Little Bit playing with the hose near the garden.

say that all the crops except radishes were calamitous failures.

Seeing that their mother was relaxed and at ease around us, the cubs soon got over their shyness. After ten days, Patti had gained enough of their confidence to be able to touch them. She had also taught them to slurp cold canned milk from a bucket on hot days, which they did with all the finesse of messy little two-year-olds in high chairs. With their paws in the milk and chipmunks running by, they had the attention span of a pair of gnats. More of the milk ended up on their coats and on the deck than in their mouths.

Even without the hose to play with, Little Bit continued to take her cubs up to the shady grass near the garden. Every afternoon, as the temperature rose, they would go up there to play. The cubs would wrestle, then Little Bit would lie on her

Little Bit nursing Winnie and Pooh.

back and they would scramble and climb all over her, nibbling on her ears. She'd bat them around gently and they would fall over and get back up.

After a while, as their energy waned, she'd pull them close to nurse. Then it would be nap time, either under the floor of the old shed or up in the gently swaying branches of the large white spruce that shaded the area.

It was heartwarming to watch Little Bit be both mother to and playmate with her cubs. The days were warm and dry, and they seemed to inaugurate what would be a perfect and magical summer. But that was before the fires began.

9

FIRE IN THE WOODS

With no moisture since the cold rains of mid-May, our new back-yard grass was soon in trouble. I finally went down to Buck's Hardware on a Saturday morning and bought a pump that would allow us to draw water from the creek for the sprinklers. It took all that day to set up the system and water the entire lawn.

That same day, the forest fires started breaking out. Lightning strikes caused two to start about ten miles northwest of us. A careless smoker lit another one near Poplar Lake. All told, eight fires were burning in the county by day's end.

In the mid- to late eighties, budworms had killed millions of spruce and balsam trees. Now falling down and rotting, the trees filled the woods with extra fuel. Dry hot weather did the rest, creating an explosive situation.

Although the public was unaware of the danger, the Forest Service had begun moving fire-response teams up the Gunflint Trail several days earlier. Now they put out the call for hotshot crews from the West Coast to supplement our own firefighters. By Monday, all the fires but two had been doused, but those two, located in the wilderness area, had each consumed more than a thousand acres. An incident command post was established, 350 firefighters arrived, and the battle was joined.

Wednesday, Patti and I awoke to find a thin haze of smoke in the woods around the house. The acrid smell of it hung in the air. I had talked to the incident commander the previous afternoon, who confirmed that the crews were having a hard time of it in the rough and isolated country. The fires were about ten miles away and burning slowly towards us.

We loaded our camera equipment into the truck and set out to have a closer look. Five miles up the Gunflint Trail we drove into heavy smoke that cut visibility to about a hundred yards. It appeared the wind had swung more to the west. We turned west on the South Brule Road and passed a hotshot crew from Idaho, dirty and red-eyed, strewn with their equipment along a ditch. A big double-rotor helicopter had landed in a smoky meadow and was off-loading firefighters whose yellow Nomex fire-retardant shirts were still clean.

We continued on to the T in the road. The fire was a mile ahead. Two bulldozers were cutting a fireline along the road. We stopped and talked to one of the operators and to an outfitter who had delivered the last of his canoes to help reach the fires more quickly by water. They told us the two fires, having connected, had grown to 6,000 acres and worked their way northeast. They had done all they could. The real effort was taking place back in the smoke-filled woods, where the fire still advanced.

We turned north and drove back out of the heaviest pall of smoke to where we could again draw a decent breath. As we neared the north fork of the Brule, we saw perhaps the most unusual sight in all our years there: two cougar kittens playing on a ledge just off the side of the gravel road.

"Did you see that?" I asked as we went by.

Patti nodded in agreement. "I can hardly believe it. Just a few years ago people were saying that cougars didn't live around here."

We slowed to a stop and backed through the gravel dust to the ledge alongside the road, where the kittens had been playing, but they were gone. We stopped the truck and opened the windows to listen for them, but there was nothing.

The idea of going into the woods to look for them occurred to us, but we talked ourselves out of it. The kittens were probably with their mother, who would certainly not appreciate our intrusion.

In the days that followed, we waited for the wind to switch back towards us, but it continued to blow out of the southwest, and we were thankful. Finally, the blaze reached a critical bottleneck. If it could be stopped there, it could be contained and put out. The commander made a bold decision. He put his top three hotshot crews directly against the head of the fire. For eighteen hours, the crews stood up against the blaze and stopped it cold. It was heroic work.

The wind did eventually shift, and the smoke again drifted back to drape itself through our woods for several days, but the immediate danger was over. Hazardous conditions would return before the summer was over.

Just as Little Bit made regular visits each day in June, Big Mama came to visit every night. Usually she waited until 10:00 P.M. or later, when dusk became darkness, to lead her trio of little cubs up onto the deck. At that time of year, real darkness only lasts from 10:30 P.M. until 4:00 A.M.—less than six hours.

At this point, each of the three weighed no more than six or seven pounds. Because they were nocturnal, their eyes looked as big as teacups. They seemed to know that their mother wanted them to make friends, and they gathered eagerly at the back door as Big Mama stood guard. While cubs that size are not as squiggly as puppies, they certainly keep busy. These climbed all over one another to give our arms a lick and to get into the seed box.

Saturday afternoon, June 20, was hot and breezy. We had a couple of fans turned on in the house to move air. Suddenly, we noticed they weren't running. That led to a check of the circuits and to the discovery that the power was off. Both of us immediately assumed the worst: a cub had climbed an electrical pole. Our wind chimes from two years earlier had fallen off and we had forgotten to replace them. Guilt welled up and spilled over.

I called the power company. Once again, ours was the only call they had received. Fortunately, the emergency crew was nearby and responded quickly. I told them of our fears and explained how it had happened two years earlier. They had heard the story.

It took only a few minutes to confirm the worst. At first, we thought it had to be one of Little Bit's cubs on the wires, because she moved them primarily by daylight. But within the hour, she arrived safely with Winnie and Pooh tagging along.

That left Big Mama and her triplets. There seemed to be no other young cubs around that summer. So we began the wait, expecting her to bring back the survivors just before dark. It did not happen. There was no sign of them, and we began to worry that some tragedy even worse than the loss of a cub had befallen them. All through the second day and evening we watched and waited, with several visits by Little Bit, but none by Big Mama.

The third night, well after 10:00 P.M., Big Mama came back with two cubs. She was jumpy and nervous, but at least she and her two little survivors looked healthy and uninjured. The following morning, they were back again for a rare daylight visit. It was another warm day, with high humidity and no wind. The mosquitoes circled relentlessly over the two cubs, who also looked like little dirtballs. In honor of Charles Schulz and his cartoon character, we named the cubs Pig and Pen.

Big Mama's babies, Pig and Pen.

One of the cubs on a duck box.

In the daylight, we discovered that one of the cubs, Pig, was a male, and the other, Pen, a female. Pig was easily the more aggressive, being downright pugnacious toward his sister. He was always the first on the deck to get seeds or affection, and the last to leave. Sometimes, he hung around for ten minutes after his mother and sister had gone. That's when we thought he'd never find them. But of course, his nose never failed him and the three were always quickly reunited.

A couple of days later, we put together three wind chimes and went from power pole to power pole, nailing them in place. These rang at the slightest bit of breeze and would certainly frighten away cubs for a while.

A few nights later, Little Bit and her cubs relaxed on the deck until it was almost dark and the stars began to come out.

Their delay in leaving led to an encounter with Big Mama and her pair that went on for an hour and a half, a seeming eternity.

Little Bit had smelled them coming. We could tell she was nervous, but with us on the deck, she felt protected and made no move to leave. She dithered around and the cubs grew restless, but they weren't able to discern what she wanted of them. At that point, Big Mama arrived. Both females huffed at each other briefly and Big Mama sat down to wait her turn at the bottom of the deck. She was about fifteen feet from the steps, ordinarily enough for Little Bit and her cubs to pass.

To get the entire picture, you have to understand that the steps were the only way up or down unless you climbed one of the posts. To this state of affairs add the uncertainty of darkness and the confusion caused by the bright beams of our flashlights. When you have two nervous, protective mothers and four cubs in close quarters in the dark, the cubs are certainly at risk. Even the normally mild-mannered Little Bit seemed to dislike strange cubs. We didn't know how the mothers would react. There was great potential here for a calamity to occur, and my heart was pounding.

Little Bit clunked to her cubs and led the way down the steps and to the left, away from Big Mama. The cubs, however, stalled at the steps, retreated, and skittered around the deck, looking for an alternate way to escape. I heard Patti give a low groan.

"Oh, oh," I said. "We've got a problem. I'll try to get Big Mama farther back, and you get the cubs down."

Big Mama waited patiently, but her pugnacious little Pig was determined to get up on the deck. I shooed him back toward his mother, who stood up, apparently agitated. When it came to those cubs, she was very protective, and I didn't want to lose that thin thread of trust she had in us. The plan that had seemed so easy to figure out, now became impossible to put into action.

With their mother down below clunking for them to come, Winnie and Pooh were confused. They just couldn't find a way off the deck. Patti finally coaxed the two babies over to the steps, but with me halfway down the steps and little Pig rampaging around below me, they saw no recourse but to do an about face, fleeing back across the deck, where they piddled in fear and climbed up to the top railing, about fourteen feet above the ground. Patti went back for another try, herding them gently along the railing, but at the steps, they again balked and retreated.

At that moment, Big Mama added to the problem by advancing to the bottom step. She was tired of waiting, and it showed. This was one of those times when we simply did not have enough manpower to keep Pig and Big Mama at bay on one side and lead the two cubs to safety on the other. We needed at least one more person.

I threw up my hands and suggested we trade places. So Patti went down and tried to convince Big Mama and Pig to back off, while I herded the two hysterical cubs along the perimeter of the bench toward the steps.

"I need the bear stick," I thought out loud. "That'll move them along." I got it and tried gently nudging them. It took a great deal more than a nudge. Pushing them along as they wetted on the bench in fear, the two reluctant cubs slid toward the steps. I think at that moment, with all my pressure and verbal commands, that I was more frightening to them than Big Mama was.

They reached the bottleneck at the bottom of the stairs and went right on through, with me pushing. Pooh went down the steps, peeled off to the left, and was soon reunited with her anxious mother. Winnie, though, got confused by the dark shape ahead and went straight for Big Mama and her cubs. My heart stopped. I didn't know what she'd do. At the last second, Winnie saw his mistake and veered left, colliding with Pig. Pig jumped for the white spruce tree and clambered up, followed by the desperate Winnie.

"Oh no," I said as my shoulders sagged in frustration. "Now we've got an even bigger mess." The male cubs were up the tree, calling frantically for help, while the two females were down hiding behind their mothers. Both mothers were clunking to order their cubs down immediately. Each cub

Pig gets ready to climb the old white spruce.

looked at the other's mother as if to say, "You can't order me around or trick me into coming down. You're not my mother."

Patti and I shrugged, not knowing this time what to do. She glanced at me and said, "Another fine mess you've got us into, Ollie." Truthfully, the way they were tangled up in the branches, there wasn't much we could try, because we didn't know how far we could push Big Mama. Then, too, we were by that time wrung out.

Finally Patti said, "I'm going in the house. Maybe they can figure things out better by themselves." And that is exactly what happened, although it took rather a long while.

First, Big Mama and Pen came up on the deck and hunkered down in the light shining out of the living room to eat seeds. Seeing them triggered Pig to slide past Winnie down the tree and join his mother on the deck. Winnie stayed up the tree, calling, and Little Bit retreated a respectable distance until Big Mama and her pair left the scene a half hour later. Then Little Bit came back and called Winnie down to end the standoff and reunite her twins.

Little Bit hated any kind of violence. She was large for a female, but almost always avoided confrontation. One night, she was leaving the deck with her cubs when two male bears arrived on the scene. Winnie had lagged behind and become separated from his mother. It was dark. He smelled the males. Like almost any cub would, he climbed the closest tree.

I went out and chased the males off the deck, hoping they would go on their way. But they went down into the woods and stopped, right by the tree that Winnie had climbed. Rather than try to chase them away, Little Bit sat for a while waiting, then called Pooh and left the area. When Winnie realized he'd been left behind, he started squalling from his tree-top perch. It was heartbreaking to hear and went on for at least twenty minutes. I was about ready to go down into the woods with a flashlight to help when Little Bit came back on the deck and clunked to him. The two males had slipped away. Her nose told her this, and she was once again in charge. Her return and her clunking reassured Winnie that all was well. He came down, and the trio went on their way. And Patti and I thankfully went to sleep.

Always big worriers, we immediately thought the worst when Little Bit and Pooh showed up without Winnie. The weather was warm and sunny, virtually windless. We walked down toward the creek and into the woods calling the little cub, but there was no sign of him.

"Where is your cub, Little Bit? Where's Winnie?" I asked, knowing there would be no answer. For her part, Little Bit seemed content and unconcerned. She made no signals we could understand or follow.

"I guess we just wait and hope for the best," I said with a shrug. "Maybe he'll show up in a few minutes." But the minutes became hours and although Little Bit seemed perfectly happy to relax in the shade, of Winnie there was no sign.

Next morning, keeping a close watch, we saw Little Bit and Pooh splash across a shallow, moving section of the creek and walk slowly up the lawn on their way to the deck. My heart sank. For a second day, there was no sign of Winnie. "I've got a bad feeling about this, but I don't know what we can do," I said.

Patti shook her head unhappily and went out with a bucket of seeds to greet Little Bit. A minute later, I heard her calling Winnie. She came rushing back into the house. "He's limping badly. I'll need some help."

For a second or two, nothing registered. "Who's hurt?" I asked.

"Winnie. He's walking across the lawn. Looks like he injured his leg somehow."

I went outside to watch Winnie hobble across the grass. He stopped at the base of the steps, weak and dispirited.

Patti hurried past with milk and seeds for the hurt cub. She sat on the lowest step and gently touched the front leg he was holding up. There seemed to be no breaks as she gently ran her hand down his shoulder and leg. Then she lifted his paw for a look.

The cub flinched in pain, and gave a startled cry. It was enough to bring a concerned mother to peer over Patti's shoulder. Reassured that her cub was in good hands, Little Bit moved back to her seed box to resume eating.

"Okay, I've got it," she said. "There's a deep cut straight across the pad. Let's get the Bacitracin."

In situations like this, her time as a vet's assistant in Florida came in handy. She knew what to do and how to do it. So I gave her the tube of antiseptic and she squeezed a liberal dose on his pad and worked it in gently, crooning to the cub as she worked.

"Probably stepped on a piece of broken glass somewhere," she said. "I just hope it doesn't get infected. So far, it looks pretty good, if we can just keep him from licking off the medicine. The worst part is hoping it will heal. Every time he puts any weight down, it will spread the wound open, not letting it close." She sat and kept her eye on the cub as he happily slurped up the milk and ate some sunflower seeds. At least his appetite appeared to be good.

When Little Bit and Pooh left, Winnie limped along behind. They went back across the rocky creek and climbed the steep hill beyond, Winnie trying gamely to follow.

When the threesome came by the next day, Winnie again remained at the bottom of the steps, not willing to risk the climb up. Again, Patti checked his foot, rubbed a little more antiseptic on, and gave him seeds. "The pad doesn't seem to be hot or swollen anymore," she noted. "So far, so good."

We watched them plod along the fence and into the woods, with Winnie again bringing up the rear. That's the last we saw of them for three days. It was blueberry season, and we knew from past experience that Little Bit was out getting a jump on what little crop there was.

Upon their return, Winnie's paw showed noticeable improvement. He was starting to put weight on it now, moving with a limp, but with greater agility. The trio came up on the back deck, and at first we thought everything was going to proceed as usual. But then we noticed a major change. Instead of deferring to her big brother, Pooh sought to establish dominance. When Winnie tried to jam his head alongside hers in the milk pail, she snapped and snarled. After a brief confrontation, which upset Little Bit, Winnie amazed us by deferring to his sister.

Little Bit hated arguments between the cubs and would try to separate them when they squabbled by pushing herself in between the two yowling cubs. They were now larger, weighing thirty to forty pounds apiece and capable of sounding rather fierce and formidable when they wanted something. For Pooh, this was a chance to be boss and she took it.

That day and the next, she tried to bully Winnie several times, hoping to set the tone. He backed away, and we thought Pooh had made her point, for the arguing subsided.

But Winnie was just biding his time. A week later, when his limp was about gone and he was apparently back to normal, Pooh took him on again, figuring he would back away. This time, he snapped and snarled right back at her until Little Bit, with guttural protests, literally wedged herself between them to end it. In these arguments, there was a great deal of noise and some pushing, but nobody was ever bitten or injured.

The squabbling went on almost every day for another week, which upset Little Bit more than either of her cubs.

Finally, Winnie reestablished a narrow dominance and the arguments subsided. As for Patti and me, we had received a valuable lesson in bear psychology.

Whenever we thought we had learned a lot about bears, they would do something so unexpected as to leave us shaking our heads in wonder. No surprise was greater than the one I got from Big Mama in early July.

Because Little Bit spent so much time on the deck during the day and Big Mama could be expected to arrive most evenings, Patti and I had taken to shooing the males off the deck. They weren't troublesome, but we wanted to keep the field clear for the mothers and the cubs. Our efforts also served to keep males from being scared witless by Big Mama when she arrived.

That particular evening, a young male had come up on the deck, just after Little Bit left with her cubs. He was lapping up seeds out of the big seed box just about the time Big Mama was to arrive. I went out, he trotted off, and I picked up the box and took it inside. A few minutes later, Big Mama, Pig, and Pen arrived. I went to the door, slid it open, and took the box back outside.

Big Mama had developed the habit of standing close and smelling my arm as I reached to set out seeds or the occasional milk bucket. So when she came over to sniff me, I paid no attention. This time, however, as I set down the box, she quietly opened her mouth and bit me on the forearm. She let go as quickly as she could before biting down hard, but still her big upper canines had deeply punctured the inside of my arm.

I stood up, more shocked than hurt, and went inside, where I said to Patti, "She bit me," in a very calm voice.

"What?" said Patti, thinking she had heard wrong. Then

she hurried into the living room, where I stood staring in amazement at the bloody rivulets running down my arm.

"That's a bad puncture," she said, grabbing a towel. We guessed it was about a half-inch square and three-quarters-inch deep. "Maybe we should go down to the emergency room to have a doctor check it out."

"No," I said firmly. "We can handle it right here. Besides, it isn't that bad. We'll just get a bandage."

She looked at me doubtfully.

I responded. "I don't want everybody in town saying, 'I told you so. I knew it was just a matter of time!' Besides, it will be fine. It was just a mistake." She had the iodine in hand and now she poured it into the open wound.

"Whoa," I said, "I can sure tell it's working." The iodine hurt more than the bite.

She let the blood run for a couple of minutes to clean the wound, then put pressure on it to slow the bleeding. "What do you mean, it was a mistake?" She asked.

I explained how I had passed the seed box, fresh with the scent of a male bear, right under her nose. "When she got a whiff of that bear, she just went into protective mode and chomped down. But she let up immediately. Never even clamped her jaws. If she had, I'd be in trouble right now. She would have gone right down to the bone. Instead, I've got one hole in the meaty part of my arm and a couple of marks from her lower teeth on the top of my forearm."

I went on to explain that Big Mama had backed away right after the bite, and had made no warning to frighten her cubs. "It was just an obvious mistake," I repeated. "A knee-jerk reaction."

"Right," she said. There was a twinkle in her eye. "Think of the story you can tell someday of being bitten by a cross-eyed half-blind bear. Very heroic."

We talked about the bears for quite a while that night. We were still talking long after Big Mama and her cubs had gone. Beyond the two females and their offspring, we had generally discouraged bear visitors. Occasionally, when one of the males from past years like Sarge wandered by, we'd welcome him, but those days were rare. Skinny and Scar were gone. Irving had left. Pretty Boy hadn't been back all summer. Adult male bears travel long distances to establish their own territories. Who knows how far our friends had gone? Other than a couple of juveniles and Honey, our only visitors were Little Bit and Big Mama. Any other bears we saw were just hungry travelers, like hobos on the road, hoping to find handouts.

I went to work the next morning with a square bandage on my arm, managing to deflect questions from co-workers by saying I'd run into a sharp branch in the woods. Within a week, the bandage was no longer necessary. The wound healed without infection and was soon ignored.

However, the scar remains a vivid reminder of that evening in July, and I still wear it with some pride. Not many people experience a black bear bite without bad memories afterward. I may even be unique in that regard.

Quite often that month, we would see Honey, the juvenile female. Generally, she'd avoid the backyard and stay out front, sneaking sunflower seeds from the birdfeeder trays. She was gangly and awkward and always a bit afraid of the other bears, but she was curious and seemed to want our company, so she stayed close.

Some bears have distinctive trademarks or habits. Honey's was a propensity to stand up on her hind legs to look around. She was always standing up to see better. Maybe she had inherited her mother's poor eyesight.

One day we were sitting on the deck with Little Bit and the

cubs when Honey made a rare appearance on the back lawn. This was one of those hot, dry days we'd been seeing often. It was not pleasant weather for big, heavy mother bears like Little Bit, and perhaps the sight of the younger female irritated her and stirred her protective instincts.

I was waiting for Honey to retreat when Little Bit decided she'd had enough of what she must have taken to be impertinence. She got up, took a look at Patti, then padded over to the steps. She walked quietly down, then took off running after Honey, leaving us to babysit the cubs. She galloped through the bushes and out onto the lawn. Honey, up on her hind legs, was probably as taken aback as we were. She dropped on all fours and ran.

"Little Bit!" Patti called. "Come on back. She won't hurt your cubs." But Little Bit was serious. I figured she would tire of running and end the chase once Honey ran into the woods.

We started talking to Winnie and Pooh, who knew us quite well and felt safe around us by now. Pooh climbed into Patti's lap, and we all patiently waited for Little Bit to give up and return. A couple of minutes later, moving at top speed, Honey emerged from the thick woods on the south side of the house. Not more than twenty feet behind was a determined but panting Little Bit. They had looped completely around the house and come out again on the lawn. At first I wanted to laugh. Here was a gazelle-like juvenile female who really had no fear of being caught by her ponderous pursuer. Indeed, Honey kept glancing back at Little Bit, who was badly winded, her pace radically slowed. Still, Little Bit kept up the chase, across the lawn and back into the woods, heading north. Then close to the deck, she abruptly stopped, sides heaving. We could hear Honey still tearing along.

Patti went over and commiserated with Little Bit, who needed a drink of water. We could actually hear her breath rasping inside of her. This was one tired bear. Still, she had accomplished her mission of removing Honey. We knew it had to be because of the cubs, one of those protective mother-bear things.

That time of summer, late July and early August, was our busiest time at the paper, and we were sometimes gone from home eight or ten hours. When that happened, Little Bit always left her calling card, muddy paw prints on the glass door. After she'd crossed the creek and the new back lawn, her wet feet would pick up some dirt, which she would then deposit on the sliders as she gently tapped a paw against the door.

Once or twice each week, Little Bit arrived early in the morning, when it was just daylight and we were still asleep. She would tap her claws just loud enough to make a distinctive clicking sound, which would awaken the light-sleeping Patti. The early mornings were cool on the shady deck, and for some reason the mosquitoes were also less voracious.

Patti spent many an early morning hour on the deck with Winnie, Pooh, and their mother that summer before work. When the bears left, they only went as far as the deep grass north of the house where they snoozed in the shade, or across the creek to their daybeds in the ferns.

Honey came back shortly after the chase and stayed in the front yard, where Little Bit rarely ventured. She was a regular from that day on until her hibernation.

As August advanced, hot and dry, the threat of fire remained perilously high. Officials were torn between the never-ending need for tourist dollars and the dangers caused by the presence of those same tourists. Finally, on a hot and windy Thursday afternoon, someone camping on the shore of a small wilderness lake near the border lit the spark that set the forest ablaze.

A snack for Little Bit and her cubs.

The Saganaga fire, as it was called, raced seven miles and consumed 9,000 acres the first day. Great clouds of gray smoke rolled across the northern sky. Traffic was turned back north of our house on the Gunflint Trail. For two weeks, the best fire-fighters in North America struggled to contain it. Twenty square miles of timber, then thirty, were destroyed.

For a week, the west wind held and the fire flowed east like molten lava into Canada. Then, with a switch in the air currents, the smoke slid south through the river valleys like a great, gauze-like serpent. When you can stand outside inhaling its pungent odor and watching its gray haze blur the air, a fire suddenly becomes pervasive. It's all you think about. How fast is it traveling? How far away is it? What are the chances for rain?

As long as the fire burned, we also feared that others might erupt. Closer to us. More dangerous. A few lightning strikes would do it. A careless smoker.

Meanwhile, the bears were on the move, looking for food across a dry, inhospitable landscape. Their favorite berries, hazelnuts, and vines, plentiful during the best of times, were now hard to find. Their search was hot and tiring and unproductive.

Even when the wind switched again and the smoke dissipated, the air was dry and gritty enough to taste. One evening, I came home from work, got out of the truck, and looked back down the driveway to see the dust still hanging suspended in the air between the trees like an uninvited presence from outer space.

At times like this, even our familiar bears started acting strangely. One day, we came home at lunchtime to find Big Mama standing on her hind legs, looking up from the back deck at the steeply slanted A-frame roof. It was the first and only time we'd ever seen her standing on two legs. Halfway up the roof, Pig clung to the shingles, his claws dug in deep. The sun had been bearing down on those shingles all morning, and they were evidently hot, because he was frightened and complaining loudly.

While this drama was unfolding, Pen enjoyed her seeds from the box, able at last to enjoy her full measure without a battle. The entire scene was incongruous. It might also have been humorous but for the danger to Pig. The roof was steep and ended with a ten- or twelve-foot drop to the ground. Why the cub had climbed halfway up the pitch and traversed at least a dozen feet to where he lay clinging was a mystery. But there he was, afraid to make a move, while his mother tried to talk him down.

After assessing the problem, we held off and stepped back. Aggressive assistance would only have driven the cub higher on the roof and made it harder for him to come down. We waited and watched, while the cub thought things through. I was reminded of reading something about a family trying to adopt a cub and bring it into the house. It didn't work because the cub was always into everything, breaking, scattering, and tearing. It was like having a two-year-old child with super strength trashing your house every day. Watching Pig, I could understand the nightmare that family had experienced. I shuddered at the thought.

"What's wrong?" Patti asked.

I told her what I had been thinking about—how a family tried to adopt a cub.

"We won't be trying *that*," came her quick reply.

Pig clung to the shingles for another fifteen minutes before his mother said some mysterious magic bear words and he started to climb down the roof toward her. As he moved, he gained confidence in his balance and the desperation in his movements ended. He got to the edge of the roof about fifteen feet above the deck, then eased himself down to where the roof ended just above the corner of the hand rail. He slid onto the railing, dropped down to the bench, and galloped over to the seed box, where he pushed Pen aside and started gobbling his lunch.

"Made it look pretty easy," I noted. "Let's hope he doesn't take to climbing up there on a regular basis."

Fortunately, he had just finished his first and last trip to the roof. We never saw another bear, including him, up there again, which was reassuring. It had been some trick for him to get up there in the first place, and we often wondered why it had occurred to him to try it.

Looking back at the summer of 1995, I am reminded of the famous quotation by Dickens, "It was the best of times. It was the worst of times."

At the office, the newspaper was going strong. At home, the mother bears and their cubs were regular companions. But far away in Oregon, Patti's dad, Alex, was succumbing to a mysterious type of cancer. We flew there over the Fourth of July to visit, and to show him pictures and a videotape of the bear he loved so much. After he watched the footage, there were tears in his eyes.

"I feel sorry for Little Bit," he said. "She won't be getting any more of my special almonds."

We poo-pooed his words, but they were prophetic. He died within a month. When the phone call came with the news of his death, I had just gone for a walk down the driveway with our dog Sheba. So Patti stepped out on the deck where Little Bit was sitting and nestled herself beside the huge bundle of fur.

When I walked into the living room, I spied Patti outside. I went out and sat down. Her arms encircled the bear's neck and she was sobbing with her eyes closed.

"What is it?" I asked quietly.

"Dad died," her words were muffled into Little Bit's coat. "I just got the call." She sat quietly with the bear for another half minute, then Little Bit leaned her massive head against Patti's. I knew she understood nothing of what was going on, but she felt something and responded. It was a magic moment in a time of grief and one I will never forget.

We were down to the last bowlful of West Coast almonds.

Little Bit's favorite treat: almonds from California.

We made certain Little Bit got all the rest, as Patti's dad would have wanted.

Shortly after that, Little Bit and her young ones left for what we thought would be another two- or three-day trip to the berry patches. The trip dragged on for several days, and we watched with dismay as hunting season edged closer. After one week, September 1 arrived and, with it, the bear hunt. There was no sign of them.

"I can't stand this any longer," Patti said. "Could we drive around the area and at least look at the berry patches we know about?"

I nodded. "Sure. I don't know if there's any hope of finding them, but we can go look. Tomorrow's Saturday. We'll start off first thing if she doesn't show up tonight." There was still no sign of Little Bit or the cubs that evening or again in the early morning. But there was shooting, and that strengthened our resolve to find our wayward bear.

The search led north, where we drove old logging roads that led to the creek, then walked across to the berry-picking areas we knew west of there. But the patches were abandoned. No berries, no hunters—and no bears. The blueberry leaves crumbled to dust in our hands.

For the bears, it was a time of terrible hunger. For the hunters and their tempting baits, easy pickings. That fall, 270 bears were killed in Cook County. It was a hellish slaughter.

We continued prowling the back roads that weekend, but we saw no bears and only a couple of hunting camps. Fortunately, they were several miles away and we hoped Little Bit would be much closer if she was still alive. But we could not find her and still she did not return. We asked our neighbors to keep a close lookout for her, but there was nothing. She and the cubs had simply vanished.

The days went by. We heard gunfire virtually every morning and evening. Finally after fourteen days, with both of us at the breaking point, Patti went out on the back deck. Clenching her fists, she looked out across the western horizon and shouted out, "God, listen to me please. Don't do this! My dad is with you, but please, please don't take Little Bit at the same time. It's too much to ask. Please let her come back. I know you're listening. Thank You."

Well, I thought, if God ever heard a prayer, He must have heard this one. But still, it had been fourteen days. If Little Bit was coming back, she would have been here by now. I gathered my wife in my arms and the tears welled up in my eyes. I was proud of her courage and determination in the face of what I was starting to think were long odds.

We went inside to fix our plates for dinner. Not more than ten minutes later, Little Bit walked onto the deck, followed by Winnie and Pooh. She walked over and looked in the sliding glass door as if to say, "Well, you called, so here I am."

We were so relieved to see her that it didn't even occur to us to notice if she looked at all different. We supposed that they had found things to eat while somehow avoiding the gauntlet of bear hunters and their temptations. We dug out all our stored-up goodies, such as honey and condensed milk, and treated the prodigal trio to a real feast.

SEPTEMBER RAINS

The second week of September brought the welcome rains we had not seen all summer. They were drenchers that soaked deep to extinguish smoldering roots and douse embedded embers glowing in lightning-struck snags.

The forest fires died out, the crews went home, and even the command center folded its tents and demobilized. It had been a hard, hot summer, and the cold rain was an unmistakable sign of its end.

Little Bit and her cubs, who by now seemed as wide as they were tall because of their fat and long fur, stayed close to the house after their two-week mystery trip. Little Bit's metabolism was slowing as she neared hibernation, but the cubs were still full of energy and kept her moving.

Late one afternoon, after a bit of pulling and tugging, the cubs managed to tip the nearly empty seed box off the edge of the deck. "Way to go, guys," Patti said, getting to her feet and heading for the stairs to recover the box.

Winnie peered over the edge to observe the seed box, while his sister turned away to look for seeds along the railing. I got up to go into the house for a minute, and at the same time Little Bit pulled herself to her feet and sauntered over to watch Patti down below.

One moment, the afternoon was quiet and relaxed, the next moment it was a blur of excitement. Events unfolded so rapidly that afterward, I could never be sure exactly in what sequence they took place. As Patti went into the bushes below the deck to retrieve the seed box, a large male bear slid silently out of the brush no more than ten feet behind her. At first, she only was aware of Little Bit racing down the steps.

She glanced up and was about to say, "Hey, what's going on?" but none of it came out except the "Hey"—at that moment Little Bit hit the big male broadside with her full force. The male bellowed as he lost his footing and went down the slope with a ferocious Little Bit riding his flank.

Patti was speechless as she watched the tumbling bears go past. Little Bit's teeth gripped the big male's shoulder. He tried to fight back, but she would not relent, driving him out onto the grass. In desperation, he turned and fled toward the creek, with Little Bit snapping angrily at his hip. He splashed through the water and plunged into the wall of yellowing leaves beyond. There, Little Bit let him go. She stood in the creek for a few seconds, listening to him and catching her breath, then slowly turned and plodded back up across the lawn. Her pace was such that you'd thought she hadn't moved any faster than a tortoise in weeks.

Patti waited down below, then put an arm around Little Bit and checked for bites. "Little Bit, you amaze me. How do you keep coming up with this stuff?"

"Unbelievable," I agreed, shaking my head.

Somehow, Little Bit had smelled or heard the approaching male. Then, when he appeared, she simply reacted instinctively to protect Patti. We don't know whether the bear meant any harm or posed any danger at all. We suspect not, but Little Bit was taking no chances.

Two years earlier, we had called her timid and uncertain. Now, after chasing Honey and driving off the male, she seemed anything but timid, although she was completely gentle and easy-going around us. She had simply matured into a confident and decisive mother bear.

As for Patti, she came up the steps with her hand over her heart. "Just when you think you understand the bears, they surprise you." She took a couple of extra deep breaths and sat down. Shaking her head, she looked at the now placid Little Bit. "What a bear! She protected me as if I were one of her cubs."

We can never know what motivated her at that particular moment. Maybe she was thinking only of the cubs on the deck. Somehow, though, I think there was more to it. Little Bit thought Patti needed help and responded. We have never gotten over the surprise of that moment, and I'm sure we never will. In that one brave act, she defined herself in our minds and hearts forever.

In mid-September, after several more late-evening standoffs with Big Mama and her cubs, Little Bit moved the center of her evening operations to the front yard. She seemed to know that as the days grew shorter, she would have more after-dark confrontations on the back deck. So one evening, she went to the front yard and began to play with her cubs beneath the tamarack tree. We went out with a seed tray and some milk, and after indulging themselves, she and the cubs seemed content to stay right there.

We were happy to see this, because untangling two mothers and four cubs every evening for a half hour or more was stressful work, for all concerned. Now, with Little Bit's change of scene, she and Winnie and Pooh could lounge around under the yard light while Big Mama and her brood held forth on the back deck.

Surprisingly, the front yard was used by Little Bit only in the evening. In the daylight hours, she still lounged around the back deck as before. We discovered this one day when we went home at noontime to see how the carpenter was doing on the combination bookcase–room divider he was installing. We arrived just as he and his helper were having lunch. They had turned around a pair of rockers in the living room and while munching their sandwiches, were enjoying a show on the back deck starring Little Bit's two cubs.

The new arrangement worked out well because during the day, Honey had taken to spending time out in front under the cherry tree, where she could find seeds. She was never present after sunset, which accommodated the needs of Little Bit. The two females may have smelled each other's presence on the front lawn, but this didn't seem to matter as long as they didn't have to share the space.

The bears were now on their annual countdown to hibernation, moving more slowly and eating less often with each passing day. Because they were wild and tuned to their own internal clocks, we had no idea when they would leave us. In fact, it was several days before we would realize they had actually gone off to hibernate and were not simply wandering about the countryside. A number of times over the years, we discovered they had been sleeping for a day or two before reawakening and returning to the house. The giveaway was the matting of green ferns laced throughout their fur.

Big Mama and her cubs last came to the deck on September 18. We did not know what had happened, only that they were

Winnie and Pooh and I, three chubbies.

gone. It was somewhat surprising, since Big Mama did not usually den early.

Then one of the fellows at work said he had heard that a mother bear with two cubs had been shot by a hunter along the power line a couple of miles east of our house. I asked when this had happened, but he said he didn't know. I asked what had happened to the cubs, but he didn't know that, either.

This was the kind of rumor I dreaded. I went into my office and sat down, feeling physically ill at the news. It couldn't have been Little Bit, but it certainly could have been Big Mama and her two cubs. We hadn't seen them for a couple of days. Of course, there was no telling how old the rumor might be. These stories tended to be told and retold, making the rounds a couple of times before fading away. Still, I had a bad feeling about it, since Big Mama had gone away suddenly, at least a week or ten days before her usual departure date.

We spent a long, hard day looking in all the likely places for motherless cubs. It was the kind of search that seldom reveals anything but that makes you feel not quite so useless just for having made the effort. Ours turned up no clues, as expected. No sign of bear hunters, either, though with grouse season now under way, shooting could be heard regularly around us most days. The numerous bird hunters tended to bring an end to the bear hunt, because their presence in the woods hampered the efforts of the bear baiters and kept the bears on guard as well.

Little Bit and family stayed on. Alone, she would have denned earlier, but the cubs delayed the inevitable. They appeared to be as full of energy as ever. One day late in the month, Patti and I were on the back deck when they splashed through the creek and romped across the lawn.

Patti laughed out loud. "Looks like a couple of kids on their way to Grandma's house for treats."

I nodded, acknowledging that she had described them perfectly. "Look at Little Bit. She's moving in slow motion.

Can't even keep up." That day and for most of the remaining days, Little Bit did not eat. She didn't even want to waste the energy needed to climb the deck stairs. She hauled herself to the lower deck and stopped just out of sight.

Patti took her a plate of sunflower seeds, but Little Bit wasn't interested. She allowed herself a few hand-fed nuts, but no more. Then she was content to stretch out like a huge dog and bask in the sunshine, leaving Patti and me to babysit the kids.

Winnie and Pooh were as fat as they could be, but continued to eat as if they were starving. They were driven by a powerful hunger common among bears in September. This hunger, coming as it does just after much of the indigenous food is gone, causes bears to travel hard looking for food and actually lose weight just before hibernation.

That evening, Little Bit stationed herself beneath her favorite tamarack tree out front. It was a quiet, bugless

Little Bit snoozing on the lower deck.

evening, so Patti and I put on jackets and went out to spend some time in the grass with her. There we sat like three old friends, while the cubs played nearby and swung like trapeze artists from the lowest limbs of the tamarack.

In the dusk, the yard light came on and bathed us in a dull white, greenish glow. Pooh came over for a quiet snuggle against her mother's side. Winnie explored the bushes just beyond the grass. Time passed, and darkness enveloped the forest. Finally, Little Bit got slowly to her feet and, without a backward glance, walked toward the darkness beyond the ring of light. The cubs fell in line and faded into the dark. I wondered if our friends were going off to hibernate.

I pondered the same question three successive evenings, but when Little Bit and company kept coming back, I stopped thinking about it. Somehow, the cubs were keeping their mother awake and on her feet. Each day, the trio arrived and departed two or three times, and ended up staying until dark.

Winnie and Pooh with Little Bit, beneath the tamarack tree.

Fat, furry, and ready to hibernate.

Late September was a golden time in other ways, as well. After the rains ended, the weather was sunny and crisp and quiet. Little Bit and her cubs kept showing up to share our evenings. Tourist season had peaked and ended. The brook trout were biting. These were borrowed days, indeed.

On September 28, we looked out to see Little Bit sitting on the back deck. Her nose, the top of her head, and front paws were all covered liberally with rust-colored dirt. She had been digging. "Getting ready, eh?" I said, bringing out a small handful of nuts for her to munch. This was the only nourishment we had seen her take for over a week.

She and Winnie and Pooh stayed on the back deck for a couple of hours. We went to sit with them until they left. In late afternoon, Little Bit got up, went down the steps, and started across the lawn. Pooh stayed close to her mother, while Winnie brought up the rear. As she reached the creek,

Little Bit stopped to wait for Winnie and turned to look back for just a moment. Patti whispered, "Go with the Lord, Little Bit." Then Little Bit led the cubs across the creek's rocky bottom and up into the shady woods. We heard them a few seconds longer. Then they were gone.

Later that fall, after all the bears had put themselves to sleep for the winter, Patti and I each wrote a couple of columns about our summer adventures with Little Bit, Big Mama, and all the cubs. We always avoided writing any stories in July, August, or September because we worried that some eager

A family portrait.

hunter might be tempted to surround our property with bear baits. Better not to remind them that we had bears around.

As always, our stories generated a lot of positive mail. A number of readers also brought in bear pictures, some of which were remarkable. One was entitled, appropriately, "Bear on a Bicycle," and another showed a bear appearing to wear a dress and standing upright. Actually, the bear had just happened to stand up behind a dress hanging from a clothesline. As for the bear on the bike, it was a cub standing on the seat of a bike leaned up against a tree, but the effect was that of an action shot of a biking bear. We ran such photos in the paper along with a few of our own, and people loved them. I honestly believe bears fascinate people because they fit so many descriptions, ranging from immense, powerful beasts to roly-poly comedians.

In mid-autumn, the deer came back as always. And when the snow started piling up in November, they migrated to Lake Superior for the winter.

This was the longest, coldest, winter in our memory, as it was on record. By late January, snow was piled head-high all along the driveway, an icy monument to what turned out to be the coldest period I had ever experienced in a lifetime of northern Minnesota winters. On five successive mornings, the two thermometers on the deck read −41, −41, −44, −34, and −43. During that stretch, an all-time low for Minnesota was recorded about eighty miles west of us, a Fahrenheit reading of minus-60 degrees.

Do you know that at minus-40 degrees, you can throw a cupful of hot coffee in the air and it will freeze and explode into an icy dust on the way down? It's true. During this bitterly cold time I often caught myself thinking about Little Bit and her cubs, hoping they were safe in a warm place beneath the snow.

One cold night, Patti and I sat before a brightly burning fire and thought back over some of the crazy happenings of past years.

We laughed about the night a bat had appeared in the house, sending Patti into hiding in a closet. She could handle bears, but not bats.

Following instructions we'd read somewhere, we turned out all the lights, opened the sliding-glass back door, and turned on the deck lights. In theory, this should have caused the bat to fly out through the open door.

That night, however, the modus operandi simply attracted a friendly bear. After waiting several minutes for the bat to escape, I looked at the open door and was shocked to discover Scar standing in it, more in the house than out, bringing with him his personal flock of several hundred mosquitoes.

Although I had little trouble getting him out of the doorway, the bat-removal plan ultimately did not work and Patti and I were kept busy for several days thereafter killing mosquitoes. The bat must have had a secret entrance, since we never saw it again.

And then there was the time Skinny and Ramah went nose to nose through the screen door on a warm summer day when the house was thrown open. Ramah was old and unflappable at the time, with questionable eyesight, and I don't think she was the least bit concerned about the big bear on the other side. As for Skinny, he simply sniffed awhile and wandered off.

After sharing several such recollections that night, we both agreed that many of our fondest memories of life in the woods had involved bears.

In mid-May, when normally the snow and ice are gone and fishing season opens, the winter that would not end still reigned supreme. The snow covered the woods to a two-foot depth. On the Saturday of the fishing opener, not a single lake in Cook County was free of ice. In fact, many die-hard anglers simply went ice fishing. The ice was reported perfectly safe in most places.

At the end of May, most of the snow and ice was finally gone and the trees were just beginning to leaf out. The deer came back up the hill. The ducks, both wood ducks and mallards, returned to their rocky posts along the creek and outwitted the deer for their share of corn.

But there were no bears. Not a single bear did we see in May. It was as though they had simply vanished. Naturally, we attributed this to the extremely late spring. Even in normal years, the mothers and their cubs did not usually return until late May or early June. This year, the change of season was a good two or three weeks late.

However, telling ourselves that the bears would naturally appear later than usual, and facing bearless day after bearless day, were two different things. June 5 rolled around, then June 10. Still no bears. That night, Patti and I sat alone on the back deck.

"What do you think?" She asked.

"I think we need to give it a little more time," I replied. "Their schedules could be quite a ways off. I don't want to start worrying when she could arrive at any time now."

"I can't help it. This time I have a really bad feeling about it."

I nodded, feeling the same fears but not being able to admit to them.

The very next day, our first bear arrived, a yearling. Within just a few minutes, we were able to identify it as Big Mama's aggressive male cub, Pig. He stayed around and Patti gave him some seeds.

"That's one," I said, holding up my index finger and hoping to sound confident.

"So where's Big Mama?" Patti asked. "Has she ever dumped her yearlings without bringing them back? No, she's never done that before."

We had no answers, only questions. The cub came back each day, and on the fifteenth, he was joined briefly by a second cub, which he chased off. We couldn't identify cub number two in the short amount of time he or she was present.

At 9:15 the next morning, a pair of adult bears arrived and made a loop of the yard. We quickly ascertained that the pair was a male and female. The female came up on the back deck, while the male waited below in the bushes. We continued watching. She seemed larger, but those eyes were a dead giveaway. It had to be Big Mama. That meant she had survived the previous hunting season after all, and had sent the cubs packing before she ever came back. She spent only a few minutes on the deck, then went down the steps where her boyfriend was waiting. They slipped through the leaves and vanished.

Two days later, two cubs showed up. A male and female, they were obviously Pig and Pen, Big Mama's yearlings. They arrived at 2 P.M. and stayed well into late afternoon.

That evening, I walked into the living room, where Patti was sitting in a rocker looking out at the setting sun. She had been crying.

"She's not coming back, is she?"

"I don't think so," I answered. "God, it's hard."

"I loved her so much," she said.

We held each other for several minutes, and I could feel Patti sobbing. There was nothing more I could say.

After six seasons with us, Little Bit had vanished.

EPILOGUE

Despite our acknowledgment that Little Bit was gone forever, we could not truly give up hope. We watched and waited, racing to the window or door at every sound, looking outside at every opportunity, but there was never any futher sign of her. Neither she nor her cubs ever came back.

Because they were wild animals, there is no way of knowing what became of them. We are quite sure they had denned successfully in the fall. But perhaps the terrible winter had been too much. Maybe they had run into trouble on the way back to our house in the spring. The wilderness can be a dangerous place, even for a bear.

It is unlikely that Little Bit awakened in the spring and decided on a different path that led away from her life with us, but maybe she somehow survived and is still out there raising babies in a distant part of the forest. There is always a flicker of that slim hope.

Late in June, Honey came back and brought us her two beautiful little cubs. For several days, we put out seeds. She was a shy bear, but seemed to be a good mother. Like Little Bit and Big Mama, she trusted us with her babies.

But the spark that Little Bit had lighted in our hearts was extinguished, taking with it our enthusiasm. We talked our feelings through, shed more tears, and reluctantly agreed that an era was over. Our summers with the bears had come to an end.

We stopped putting out seeds, and by mid-July, the yearling and Honey and her cubs had faded back into the forest.

Honey with her two cubs.

The bears continue to travel along Elbow Creek as they always have. For a few, the passages may rekindle memories of those carefree days spent on our lawn or back deck. In others, the distinctive heritage of Little Bit or Big Mama will still play a role in shaping their personalities.

None of these experiences would have been possible without Little Bit, who came as a friendly yearling and stayed to share the fullness of her life with us. Through her came Skinny, Scar, Big Mama, Pretty Boy, Sarge, Honey, Napoleon, Miracle, Pig, Pen, Winnie, Pooh, and many more with and without names, each of them distinct and unique.

Though we gave much in the way of time and trust to nurture our relationship with the bears, we received much more in return. Black bears are intelligent and complex creatures. Earning their confidence and trust was a special reward we will always treasure.

FAMILY TREES

Big Mama — born 1987 or before

Two unnamed cubs 1991

Napoleon & Honey 1993

Pig & Pen 1995

Two unnamed cubs 1996

Little Bit — born 1989

Miracle 1993

Winnie & Pooh 1995

ABOUT THE AUTHOR

Jack Becklund is a native of Minnesota. He started his career in advertising and became a newspaper editor and publisher. He now lives in Florida with his wife, Patti, their four cats, and their dog.